NATIONALISM, TRANSNATIONALISM
DIASPORIC EXPERIENCE IN BAPSI SIDHWA AND CHITRA BANERJEE

NATIONALISM, TRANSNATIONALISM
DIASPORIC EXPERIENCE IN BAPSI SIDHWA AND CHITRA BANERJEE

By
Dr. Pradnya Deshmukh
Assistant Professor
Dept. of English
Pandit Jawaharlal Nehru, Mahavidyalaya
Aurangabad (Maharashtra)
(India)

DISCOVERY PUBLISHING HOUSE PVT. LTD.
NEW DELHI-110 002

Published by:
Tilak Wasan

DISCOVERY PUBLISHING HOUSE PVT. LTD.
4383/4B, Ansari Road, Darya Ganj
New Delhi-110 002 (India)
Phone : +91-11-23279245, 43596064-65
Fax : +91-11-23253475
E-mail : discoverypublishinghouse@gmail.com
sales@discoverypublishinggroup.com
parul.wasan@gmail.com
web : www.discoverypublishinggroup.com

***First Edition:* 2013**

ISBN: 978-93-5056-285-7

Nationalism, Transnationalism
Diasporic Experience in Bapsi Sidhwa and Chitra Banerjee

Printed at:
Dynamic Printers
Delhi

Preface

This book has taken a long time in the making. This long journey has been period of interaction, scholarly discussion, exchange of ideas, views and research. Literature of Diaspora depicts the spirit of globalize era. In the age of globalization, scientific and technological advances have changed our life beyond our imagination. Migration within country and out side the country has become inevitable part of our life. Changes in the world since 1989 have refocused attention on the displaced person, the Diaspora and the people dispossess and separated from their identity and their history. Diaspora is not new: it has its roots in history and religion. Hence this particular area has innate national, international and interdisciplinary relevance over a period of time and now it has become a burning issue. When people cross the national boundary and enter the other nation, their language and culture are transformed as they come in to contact with other language and culture. The Diasporic writing raises questions regarding definition of "home" and "Nation". "Where are you from? To which country you belong?"... Answers to these questions are ambiguous today. In the age of globalization the concept of "nation" has to be redefined with reference to the theory of Hybridity and Multiculturalism.

This book focuses on Diasporic experiences of Chitra Banerjee and Bapsi Sidhwa. They critically analyze contemporary issues such as Nationalism, Transnationalism, Hybridity and cultural dislocation from women's perspective through their fiction. Their novels are explorations of contemporary histories-western, sub-continental and contemporary societies that are in state of transition. The literature of Diaspora which is emerging rapidly is the need of time as it helps to develop the skills of assimilation among the migrants all over the world.

I hope this book will make significant contribution to the cultural studies, Indian Diaspora and contemporary Bollywood, Hollywood cinema. This book is bound to prove valuable for academicians, students and researchers.

I am thankful to the editor and team of Discovery Publishing House Pvt. Ltd. for publishing this book.

Pradnya Deshmukh-Kale

Acknowledgements

I express my deep sense of gratitude to Dr. A. G. Khan, Professor of English and Director of B. C. U. D. Dr. Babasaheb Ambedkar Marathwada University, Aurangabad under whose guidance I have completed my Ph.D. I am thankful to him for his patience and the faith, which he has shown in me. I want to express my deepest thanks to Late Mrs. Khan for her hospitality and encouragement. The serenity and humility in her has given me a spiritual strength. I am thankful to Department of English, Dr. Babasaheb Ambedkar Marathwada University Aurangabad for their cooperation and encouragement

I wish to put on record my gratitude to the Librarian and staff of ASRC, CIEFL, Central University Hyderabad; Dr. Babasaheb Ambedkar Marathwada University; Vasantrao Naik College, Aurangabad; JES College, Jalana and Pandit Jawaharlal Nehru Mahavidyalaya, Aurangabad. I am thankful Dr. K. V. Kale's research group especially, Dr. R. R. Manza and Dr. Vikas Humbe and Dr. Arjun Mane for their co-operation.

I am deeply grateful to Shri. Ranghnathji Kale (President, Ajintha Education Society, Aurangabad) and Shri Prakashji Kale (Secretary, Ajintha Education Society, Aurangabad) or their cooperation and encouragement. They have helped to make my dream of book a reality. I am thankful to Shri. D. B. Chaudhari for his administrative support.

Deep thanks go to sister of my heart Dr. Prapti Deshmukh who is always with me in this guest of knowledge. My friends Mrs. Jayashri Nayak, Mrs. Sandhya Yerme, Mrs. Anjali Kumbhojkar, Nilofar Shakir and Dr. Vibha Rathod have helped me in scholarly discussion. Thanks to them.

I will be always deeply indebted to my father Mr. D. A. Deshmukh (Rtd. Principal) and my mother Mrs. Sushila Deshmukh (Rtd. Teacher) for their blessings and developing love for knowledge in me. I am thankful to my in-laws, relatives, well wishers for their kind support. Special thanks go to my sister-in-law Rajeshri Manish Pawar (USA) who has shared her diasporic experience to me, which I found useful in my research work. Thanks to my children Prajakta, Saurabh and Shalaka, for taking my care like parents during these years. Because of their high tolerance level and maturity I could give justice to my writing.

Sincere thanks to my husband Dr. K. V. Kale (Professor and Head, Department of Computer Science and Information Technology, Dr. Babasaheb Ambedkar Marathwada University, Aurangabad) who not only encouraged me but also helped in bringing my matter on paper. I want to dedicate this book work to him.

Dr. Pradnya D. Deshmukh-Kale
Assit. Professor, Dept. of English,
Pandit Jawaharlal Nehru College,
Aurangabad (MS)-431005.
Mail: pradnyakale.08@gmail.com
Cell : +91-9422206282

Contents

Preface

1. Introduction ... 1
2. Nationalism, Transnationalism, Liminality: Diasporic Experience in Bapsi Sidhwa ... 46
3. Nationalism, Transnationalism, Liminality: Diasporic Experience in Chitra Banerjee Divakaruni ... 86
4. The Narrative Art of Bapsi Sidhwa and Chitra Banerjeee ... 132
5. Conclusion ... 166

Index ... 177

Chapter 1

Introduction

Early South Asian Literature has been dominated largely by male writers like R. K. Narayan, Mulkraj Anand, Raja Rao, Nirad Chaudhari and more recently, V. S. Naipaul, Salman Rushdie, Amitav Ghosh, Shashi Tharoor, Vikram Seth, and Uppamanyu Chatterjee. Early women writers included Anita Desai, Nayantara Sahagal, Attia Hossaian, and Ruth Prawor Jhabvala. Since the 1980's a number of new writers have come up, who are often included in publication like the **New York** special issue or in Rushdie's recent anthology. The first significant fact about this "new" fiction is that the number of Indian English novels published during the last two decades easily surpasses the total output for any corresponding period earlier. But according to M. K. Naik:

> But sheer quantity, of course, does not automatically guarantee quality; hence attention must also be drawn to the increasing recognition and respect the new novelist are winning in the literary world today (1)

One obvious aspect of this recognition is the fact that far more Indian English writers are now being published abroad than ever before and their publishers include prestigious firms on both sides of the Atlantic: Faber and Faber; Andre Deusch; Heinemann; Alfred knopf; Random House. Equally remarkable is the fact that today even a young Indian writer publishing his first novel is readily accepted by leading publishers abroad. The new novelists have proved their mettle by winning, in competition with writers whose mother tongue was English, several major literary awards, prizes and distinctions, a complete list of which will occupy many pages. To note only the most outstanding of these, the two new novelists have won the Booker's Prize, supposedly the British equivalent of the Nobel Prize. Salman Rushdie for *Midnight's Children* in 1981 and Arundhati Roy for *The God of Small Things* in 1997. Similarly, Rohinton Mistry's *Such a Long Journey*, which was short listed for Booker's Prize received the Commonwealth Writers Prize for the best book. Vikram Seth also received the Commonwealth Writers Prize for the best book in 1994 for *A Suitable Boy*. And more recently Jhumpa Lahiri created history in becoming the first Indian author to win the prestigious Pulitzer Prize in the USA for her collection of short stories, *The Interpreter of Maladies (1991)*.

Born and brought up in the post-colonial world, the new novelists, many of whom are a part of the great Indian Diaspora, had no reason to feel self-conscious in handling the English language, which for them, carries no colonial baggage; it is for them simply a tool which they have mastered thoroughly with typical Indian flair for languages. They never feel the necessity of appending to their novels an annotated list of Indian words in the text, explaining their meaning. The inference is clear: earlier, the Indian writer was supposed to go at least half way to meet his reader. His successor today expects his readers to go all the way to meet him.

The new novel differs from the old in another respect also. It is far more 'globalized' in many senses. Mulkraj Anand, R. K. Narayan and Raja Rao have all lived in the west for a time, but their primary engagement has mostly been with India But the new novelists go much further. Vikram Seth sets the scene of his *The Golden Gate* in the USA and all his characters are American. In the collection of short story *Arranged Marriage (1995)*, Chitra Banerjee Divakarani sets the scene in USA and India. Further more a modern global fictional trend Viz. Magic Realism has been a potent influence on the work of new novelist. Though the new novelists do not seem to follow any of the "Big Three", their affinities are rather with that maverick of Indian English fiction: G. V. Desani's *All about H. Hatter*, an exciting amalgam of fantasy, the absurd, comedy, satire and linguistic pyrotechnics. These fictional values dominated post-colonial and post-modern fictions especially after the rise of Magic realism. M. K. Naik rightly points out:

> The Younger novelists are thus citizens of "*cyberspace*", though the ties that bind them to their motherland continue to be strong. (2).

Recent women writers from South Asia have been put into two kinds of "camps", one, indigenous writer from India, Shri Lanka, and Pakistan and two, South Asian American writers. In any bookstore in a large American city, the number of titles by writers from the Indian Diaspora makes a vivid impression. The writers include veterans like Anita Desai, Bharti Mukherjee and Bapsi Sidhwa, who have been publishing for about two decades and the one who have been around for less than half decades. In the last half decades writers of Indian origin have appearing with clockwork regularity on the literary horizon. Chitra Banerjee Divakaruni, Anjana Appachana, Bharti Kirchner, Sujata Massey, Indira Ganeshan, Shauna Sing Baldwin and of course, the Pulitzer award winner Jhumpa Lahiri add to the list of writers of Indian Diaspora. Women writers of Indian Diaspora have created a big impact in India and abroad recent time's more than male writers. Whatever may be the reason but in numbers and output, women writer have taken lead. Chitra Banerjee clearly does not believe in number game. She is not impressed by the fact that there are more Indian American women writers than their male counterparts. But what impresses her, says the best selling novelist is that

> There is an out-burst and all of a sudden there are many Indian American writers who say in loud print that we have been waiting to say for a long time. (3)

Echoing Divakaruni's thought, Marina Budho's adds that women writers of Indian Diaspora, "tell stories from a perspective that is seldom fully explored. There is a kind of hunger for these stories". (4) Another powerful reason for the success of female writers according to Budho's is:

> For many writers the literary journey will take place outside his home, but for female writer, typically the story takes place in the context of family. And women readers love to pour such a book and see how these writers explore not only multiculturalism and cultural clashes but also such taboo subjects as incest. **(5)**

India is the third largest Diaspora, next only to the British and Chinese. The migration of Indians has been gradual but relentless. One should think of it as a reverse colonization. During the Raj Indians were sent as indentured labour to various countries. Today their children are holding key-posts in almost every field. Today 22 millions strong Diaspora is living in 135 countries and is looked upon as vibrant, new face of India. Indian Diaspora has surmounted the pangs of dislocation to become the people of the world by thrift, networking skill, ingenuity, and industry. Late astronaut Kalpana Chawala was awarded "Pravasi Bhartiya Samman", for epitomizing Indian values overseas. The celebration of Bhartiya Pravasi Divas from the Year 2003 has proved that Indian Government has realized that Indian Diaspora is not "The Brain Drain" but "The Brain Gain" and huge potential resources for the development India.

Migration of people across the globe is an inseparable part of human history. Diaspora is not new; it has its roots in history and religion. Exile can be a process of rehabilitation as well as an exile into the wilderness. Our epic literature gives examples of different kinds of exile. Rama enters into it in conformity with the highest ideals of conduct; the Pandavas as punishment and for survival Indian emigration has been taking place for centuries but never before in history, India witnessed such massive movements of people from India to other parts of the world as in the 19th and 20th centuries. Exile, refugee, immigrant, expatriate and before these slave and indentured labour are words used to describe different kinds of mobility and shifts of population. They raise innumerable questions related to identity, status and power structures. But increasingly the terms, which are gaining popularity, are 'expatriate' and 'diaspora': The word 'diaspora' is literally a scattering, carrying within it the ambiguous status of being both an ambassador and a refugee. While one requires the projection of one's culture and the ability to enhance its understanding, the other seeks refuge and protection and relates more positively to the host culture. Further categories emerge through the use of such words as immigrant, exile and refugee. Their use attempts to give some indication of the ideologies choices, reasons and compulsions, which may have governed the act of migration. The 'immigrant' defines a location, a physical movement and forward-looking attitude. The 'exile' indicates a compulsory isolation and a nostalgic anchoring in the past. The word exile evokes multiple meanings, which cover a variety of relationships mother-country-alienation, forced exile, self imposed exile, political exile and so on. In Indian context almost all meanings are true with the migratory movements having been governed by different reasons at different times of history, and different reasons even contemporaneously.

In terms of the magnitude of the emigration and its spread, the European colonization, marked by the penetration of mercantile capitalism in Asia, was the most crucial phase in Indian Diaspora. Tinker provides one of the most comprehensive surveys of the emigration of Indian labour overseas during the colonial era. Broadly three distinct patterns of Indian emigration are identifiable in this period: (1) Indentured emigration, (2) Kangani and maistry labour emigration, and (3) 'passage' and 'free' emigration. A new and significant phase of emigration began after India became independent in 1947. According to Jairman J.N.:

> Broadly three patterns of emigration can be identified in the postcolonial emigration. (1) The emigration of Anglo-

Indians to Australia and England. (2) The emigration of professionals to the industrial advance countries like the USA, England and Canada. (3) The emigration of skilled and unskilled labors of West Asia (6).

The economic reasons governed the movement of indentured labour and of the trading communities; they have also governed the persuit of higher standard of living. The opportunities for work, research and freedom have motivated migration.

With regard to Diasporic literature a whole new set of question arises. Expatriate writing in its theory and practice is the work of the exile that has experienced unsettlement at the existential, political and metaphysical levels. Writers living abroad live on the margins of two societies and people who live on the margins are creating cultural theory. Language and culture are transformed as they come into contact with other languages and cultures. Diasporic writing raises questions regarding definitions of 'home' and 'nation'. Schizophrenia and nostalgia are often the preoccupation of these writers as they seek to locate themselves in new cultures. Cultures travel, take root or get dislocated and individuals internalize nostalgia or experience amnesia. The multiculturalism in India has helped Indian Diaspora to settle in an unknown land successfully. Bhikhu Parekh has observed that the Indian Diaspora is one of the most varied, representing "half a dozen religions.... seven different regions of India.... nearly a dozen castes" **(7)** It has shown great mobility and adjustability as it has often been involved in a double act of migration from India to West Indies and from there to metropolitan centre; from India to Africa and then Europe or America on account of social and political reasons. Parekh also comments upon their networking with each other, thei. sense of solidarity, which reverse the concept of 'homelessness'. The Diasporic Indian is "like the banyan tree, the traditional symbol of the Indian way of life, he spreads out his roots in several soils, drawing nourishment from one when the rest dry up. Far from being homeless, he has several homes, and that is the only way he has increasingly come to feel at home in the world". (8)

It is imperative to realize that any migration, whether made out of personal choice or out of necessity, results in a dislocation, which is always painful. The pain of the dislocation can never be ignored whether the move is forced or voluntary. It is migrant's response and reaction to his migration that colors his writing. Diasporic experiences are changing with the passage of time K. Sachidanand points out:

> There has been a tremendous quantitative and qualitative change in the phenomenon of diaspora owing to the great demographic upheavals of the last century, especially its last decades due to the unprecedent growth of the technologies of communication. (9)

The new speed, reach and dimension of communicating network including dimensions of vision, sound and movement have changed the nature of the experience of exile. It is no more solitary experience in most cases but a shared experience. Arjun Appadurai and Anthony Smith have also pointed out:

> How large communication networks erode national boundaries even as they promote intense interaction between members of Diasporic communities: but these communities remain local and provincial even as they acquire transnational characteristics. The homeland becomes at once remote and accessible due to the contradictory phenomena of migration and cyber communication. (10)

The general assumption regarding the diaspora writer is that he occupies a second space, of exile and cultural solitude. But Homi Bhabha calls it a third space. Sura P. Rath calls 'Trishanku' in his article 'Home(s) Abroad: Diasporic Identities in Third Spaces'. Both are right in explaining the exact position of diaspora people. They are outsiders for their own country and the country where they have shifted.

Sura P. Rath refered to Trishanku, a king in the Hindu epic *The Ramayana* to explain how the diaspora is a third space:

> In this obsession with going to the heaven with his own body, Trishanku represents the consequence of narcissism; his story includes an encounter between the divine and the human, and the creation of an intermediate virtual space between earth and heaven, but above all it highlights the dichotomy between body and spirit. The sage Viswamitra enables king Trishanku to ascend to heaven in/with his own body, but Indra, the king of gods, returns him back to earth to protect the integrity of gods land. As the king falls headlong down through the ethereal space, Viswamitra freezes him and builds virtual heaven with its own pantheon of gods and angels. The sage is later pacified by a repentant Indra, but Trishanku remains in his third space. Indeed he is that third space. (11)

Sura P. Rath defines diaspora as a transplanted Indian in the United States. He sees himself as a colonizer as well as a colonized. He is conscious of his postcolonial blood:

> Perhaps in me, as in thousands of other immigrants of Diaspora who inhabit the third space, live the third culture and shape the third history, post colonialism has come full circle, and the trauma of postmodernism has a final relief. (12)

Homi K. Bhabha sees individual and local experiences of Diaspora writers as a part of the larger processes of historical change. Bhabha is more concerned with instability, which at some point defines the expatriate self. Bhabha transforms the diaspora scattering to a gathering:

> Gatherings of exiles and émigrés and refugees, gathering on the edge of 'foreign' cultures; gathering at the frontiers; gathering in the ghettos or cafes of city centres; gathering in the half-life, half-light of foreign tongues, or in the uncanny fluency of another's language; gathering the signs of approval and acceptance, degrees, discourses, disciplines; gathering the memories of underdevelopment, of other worlds lived retroactively; gathering the past in ritual of revival; gathering the present. (13)

Thus Bhabha shifts the focus Nationhood to culture, from historicity to temporality; a hybridity, which cannot be, contained either in hierarchical or binary structure, Bhabha questions the historical certainty and settled nature of the term 'nationalism'. The focus of temporality provides a perspective on:

> The disjunctive forms of representation that signifies a people, a nation, or a national culture. It is neither the sociological solidity of these terms, nor their holistic history that gives them the narrative and psychological force that they have brought to bear on cultural production and projections. It is the mark of the ambivalence of the nation as a narrative strategy – and an apparatus of power – that it produces a continual slippage into analogous, even metonymic, categories, like the people, minorities, or 'cultural difference' that continually overlap in the act of writing the nation. What is displayed in this displacement and repetition of terms is the nation as the measure of the liminality of cultural modernity. (14)

Ambivalence is the precondition of the national culture. Idea of nation as an autonomous and sovereign form of political rationality is questionable. The structure of cultural liminality of the nation-space would ensure that no political ideologies could claim transcendent or metaphysical authority for themselves. With reference to the space of liminality, Bhabha points out:

> The nation is no longer the sign of modernity under which cultural differences are homogenized in the 'horizontal' view of society. The nation reveals, in its ambivalent and vacillating representation, the enthnography of its own history and opens up the possibility of other narratives of the people and their difference. (15)

According to Foucault, liminality of the nation-space removes the threat of cultural difference. The great contribution of Foucault's last published work is to suggest that people emerge in the modern state as a perpetual movement of 'the marginal integration of individual's.

Foucault raises the ethnographic question……. 'What we are today'? (16) to the West itself to suggest that the 'reason of state' in the modern nation must be derived from the heterogeneous and differentiated limits of its territory.

According to Bhabha it is to the city that the migrants, the minorities, the Diasporic come to change the history of the nation. It is the city which provides the space in which new social movements of the people are played out and new subjectivities are born. Bhabha points out:

> …It is from those who have suffered the sentence history- subjugation, domination; diaspora, displacement – that we learn our most enduring lessons. (17)

No one can doubt the enduring values of the Diasporic experience as a spring of agonized inspiration, multiple identities, new subjectivities, creative memories and fresh perspective on language and life. A time has come to problematise the concept of diaspora as it changes the history of nation. Diasporic experiences are very poignant and as they give birth to new subjectivities, creativities – they interrogate western values and traditional values.

In *The Location of Culture,* Homi Bhabha has called this third space; a hybrid location of antagonism, perpetual tension, and pregnant chaos. K. Sachidanand has rightly pointed out:

> The products of this hybrid location are results of a long history of confrontations between unequal cultures and forces, in which the stronger cultural struggles to control remake, or eliminate the subordinate partner. (18)

Writers like Gayatri Spivak, Amartya Sen, Chitra Banerjee, Bapsi Sidhwa take full advantage of their status. They did not have to burn the bridges with their past like the earlier Diaspora who were running away from religious and other political or social persecution. Several Indians migrated to America after 1970 – in search of a better life, greater promises of prosperity and material success. In the case of academics who teach in south Asian department, they had to strengthen the connection with their own country. The new immigrant was a new kind of colonizer, taking full advantage of the war-time labour market, at the same time having no intention of ruling over the land. They had a home to go back to and an identity to protect. Language, class and gender also count diasporic experience. The diasporic experience is also gendered experience when it comes to the writing of Indian women's abroad; say Meena Alexander, Panna Naik, Chitra Banerjiee, Bapsi Sidhwa, Anita Desai, Bharti Mukharjee, Jhumpa Lahiri and others.

According to Bharti Mukharjee Asian women handle expatriation very admirably and adapt their new cultures with greater ease as they are trained to please, trained to be adaptive wives and that adaptability is working to the women's advantage when they come over as immigrants. Uma Permeshwarn (Canada) also provides a much-needed gender perspective to the whole discourse. Women have ability to relate to two homes simultaneously. Perhaps women, with century of cultural indoctrinations and expectations are able to adapt more quickly and to accept and love homes without conflict or ambivalence. Literary texts of Indian Diaspora have tend to focus more on the under side of the enormous experience of expatriation, alienation and transplantation. According to Uma Permeshwaran, writers tend to focus on the pains of discrimination and alienation, because "our sweetest songs are those that tell of saddest thought". (19)

Editors often select these poignant experiences, which is momentary flare of intense emotion or thought. There is another aspect that is more inflammatory, and needs closer studies. According to Uma Permeshward the only literary work that has taken celebratory angle is Bharti Mukharjee's *Jasmine.* There are other women writers who accept that they got more space, time and freedom for writing. Diasporic writers should write about the loyalties, immigrants have for their adapted land. That's why Uma Pereshwaran writes an essay, "Home is where your feet are, and may your heart be there too!" She realized there might be writers writing other aspects of life. As publishers look for marketability, reviews and editors tend to, highlight the victim or exotic syndromes in work by Diaspora writers.

The minority majority status too contributes to the intensity of Diasporas of experience. The experience of the second generation or third generation migrant is very different from that of first generation migrant: home is just a space of imagination rather than of nostalgic recollection. They reconstruct their home land from fragments of gathered hearsay or from the Internet and create their own "Imaginary homelands" (20) K. Sachidanandan has rightly pointed, "for them home is not a place to return to, but a place to fantasize about, or may be to visit some time as a guest or a tourist" (21). The first generation immigrant's carefully cultivated values of an Indian culture which contrasted sharply against the stereotypes of "Western" culture; a culture, which in their minds was degenerate. They thought the nationalistic values inherited from an old country are vital for their survival in a new, alien land. The second generation Asians constantly tries to negotiate their allegiance to their parent's natal culture and the culture of their adopted home. In number of cases, migrants do seek to become part of the host society and over a period of time their self-identification as immigrants fades, though they may retain an ethnic identity. People who feel displaced uprooted from the native cultural tradition and who try to invent or revive a connections with a prior home often use the language of Diaspora. The Diaspora within, experience the same pangs of alienation and solitude. According to K. Satchidamnand,

> O.V. Vijayen, M. Mukundan, Kakkanandan, M.P. Narayana Pillai, Sethu, Kamala Das, Punathil Kunhabdulla, Paul Zacharia: all these pioneers of the new fiction lived, at least in their formative years as writers, in cities outside kerala, experiencing an alienation, a solitude, a torment of the absurd and the irrational and an existential angst as intense and as creative as that of say, Kafka, Beckett, Sartre or Albut camus, (27)

Expatriate writer as he moves from one culture to other culture may need to locate himself afresh in relation to the center. Writers living abroad live on the margins of two societies and people who live on the margins are today creating cultural theory. When we focus on diasporic writing some questions crop up regarding centre and margin – do the margins expand themselves and does the center shift? Does theory emanate from the intervenstions of marginal voices, or is it that their voices are controlled and homogenized by the centre? Gurubhagat Singh looks at the different ways Edward Said and Homi Bhabha approach this question. Said takes note of schizophrenic nature of the expatriate's reality and "crossing over" from one culture to another which may be a liberating experience. Bhabha transforms the Diasporic scatering to a gathering. According Edward Said:

> An exile in his battle against the meta-centre can use his mini but distinctly grounded cultural-historical centre as an ornament to liberate. Using small identity to 'privilege' one self or one's community over others is not creative; it is for that reason that this identity is to be refused. (23)

For Said though exile is constantly disagreeable or "dyspepsic", he gets "pleasure" in his venture. (Said 1994:407) At the end of his work *Culture and Imperialism* that he published in 1993, he quotes a 12th century monk from Saxony Hugo of St. Vicar where he elaborates the journey of the exile from his "homeland" to the globe. The exile first becomes "tender" then strong, and finally perfect. Said writes:

> The person who finds his homeland sweet is still a tender beginner, we to him every soil is as his native one is already strong, but he is perfect to whom the entire world is a foreign place. (24).

In the last paragraph of his book Said says:

> There seems no reason expect fear and prejudice to keep insisting on their separation and distinctiveness as if that was all human life was about. Survival in fact is about the connection between things....(25)

Gurubhagat Singh has rightly pointed: "Said' ends up at a Bhakhtinian kind of heteroglossal dialogue of different identities in which they connect with each other and become hybrids."(26) In Said's view, the small identity tends to separate and privilege itself and thereby alienates from the inter- community mosaic. Said's exile appears to be moving form hybridity to heteroglossia of the world.

For Naipaul, exile is an experience of pain, isolaton, fultility and division. Naipaul transforms his sensibility to a perpetual homelessness while Bissoondath, rejecting the homogenization of ethnicity, projects immigration as "essentially about renewal,"(27) about change. Rushdie's view is exactly opposite where in the migrant seeks to assimilate into the metropolis. Naipaul's position can therefore be termed as 'eternal exile, while Rushdie's can be called 'permanent migrancy'.

Like Rushdie, expatriate women novelists from Indian subcontinent are in a state of 'permanent migrancy' and they transform the pain of dislocation in to a celebration where exile, though painful, helps to discover new territories of experience. They, like Rushdie, rewrite their nations using the fragments of memory that they have and create their own "Imaginary homeland".(Rushdie-1991) Rushdie refers to the Diaspora as "translated" men, a fact which affects the relationship of the Diaspora with history, homeland and self. In "**Imiginary Homelands**" he writes:

> To be an Indian writer in this society is to face, every day, and problems of definition. What does it mean to be 'Indian' outside India? How can culture be preserved without being ossified? How should we discuss the need for change within our community and ourselves without seeming to play into the hands of our racial enemies? What are the consequences, both spiritual and practical, of refusing to make any concessions to western ideas and practices and turning away from the ones that came here with us? These questions are all a single, existential questions: How are we to live in the world? (28)

The Diaspora is often engaged in a balancing act in which the history of relationships between the culture of origin and of adoption also plays a role. Expatriate women novelists' re-writing of the histories of their nations are distinctly marked by the female perspective, and is different from the nations created by their male counter parts'. Their novels are representative of sub continental women producing viable cultural products; narratives that at once declare their presence and difference. They use the idea of the western feminist movement and modify those to evolve a kind of "Womanism". Their texts are not frontal attacks on the patriarchy present in their homelands. According Makrand Paranjape, they write of communities and nations not only with nostalgia or displacement but they critique and review the contemporary history and culture of their nations from objective point of view of expatriation. These novels emphasize and celebrate the women's perspective and authority as the carrier and creator of culture and history. Their novels are explorations of contemporary histories – Western and Sub continental and contemporary societies that are in state of transition.

Contemporary women writers of Indian diaspora have chosen narrative strategies like the autobiography and the quest novel to give shape to an identity grounded in these diverse experiences of expatriations and self-definition. Bharati Mukharjee falls into the trap of "Cosmopolitansim" and 'Pluralism". To celebrate cosmopolitanism as advocated by Mukharjee is to divest oneself of a historical past, and to casually repudiate histories of oppression. She assists her work to be part of the "ethnic and gender fractured world of contemporary American fiction"(29) Novelists like Meena Alexander, Bapsi Sidhwa and Chitra Banarjee do not claim to be " cosmopolitan". They are wholly preoccupied with their roots in Asia and show a marked national consciousness, constantly invoking images of their lands from memory.

According to Latha Rengachari, writers like Chitra Banerjee, Meena Alexendar etc. historicize their existence and the existence of other women in their Asian societies, without dismissing the impact of colonialism or understanding the threat of neocolonial projects. These women expatriate novelists also show a keen historical consciousness. Their approach, attitude and treatment of history are different from those of men. They study exploitation, which is limited not merely to political power, but as it invades other spheres of life- the men who abuse women, religious movements which harass the public, home, workplace, academic departments which exploit students. The conflictual layers of their narratives are inter-linked with the historical structures. Both cultural and political processes go into the making of history in these novels. Jasbir Jain points out:

> Traditional history and its male centered causation is rejected by these writers and it is in this sense that they feminize history- in their freedom from controlled vision of hegemony. (30).

These women writers are similar to Rushdie who creates 'imaginary homelands' from shards of memory (Rushdie – 1991). They know they can never be totally mainstreamed into their new world because they carry the fragments of their Asian homes into the new homelands. To substantiate this unbreakable connection to the homelands and to reinforce the expatriate's commitment to her roots, Bapsi Sidhwa writes in "Third World, Our World":

> I have no identity outside my culture. I am not a writer unless I voice the aspirations, humour, travails and reality of the only people I know well. And despite all that is wrong with my country, I cannot help temporing my criticism with compassion. I am nothing if I am not of some worth in my own part of the world my world, the third world. (31)

Bapsi Sidhwa is a well-known writer from Pakistan whose fiction has won fame both at home and places of the South Asian Sub-Continent. The Parsee novelists in English generally fall into two categories: stay-at-home writers and expatriates. Dina Mehta and B.K.Karanjia is stay-at-home novelist who deals with westernized Parsee life whereas Farrukh Dhondy,

Firdaus Kanga, Rohit Mistry, Ardashir Vakil and Boman Desai are expatriate writers. Bapsi Sidhwa's position is singular among Parsee writer as she divides her time between Pakistan and America. Bapsi Sidhwa enjoys her expatriate experience though her roots continue to exist in Pakistan. Though the experience of exile plays an important role in her writing, she has not really experienced the pangs of expatriation. Sidhwa told Chelva Kanaganayakam:

> I have not really experienced exile. I have chosen to be in America. The minute I feel like an exile, I go back to Pakistan. I have been lucky to be able to do that. And don't feel exiled in Pakistan as such. (32)

This is an advantage, which very few expatriate novelists enjoy.

Though the novel has not been a particular popular genre with the Pakistani creative writers, the presence of outstanding novelist as Ahmed Ali and Zulfiker Ghose indicates the standards of excellence. But it was Bapsi Sidhwa who gave a distinct identity to Pakistani novel in English. As there was no tradition either of women's literature or of English language literature in Pakistan at the time when Sidhwa started writing, she may be considered a pioneer in both the fields. Bachi Karkaria has rightly pointed out:

> She is the Grand dame of south Asian Anglophone writing: if Salman Rushdie is midnight, then Bapsi Sidhwa is 9 p.m. Her *The Crow Eaters* (1978) was published three years before Rushdie's *Midnight's Children*. But, she has also suffered the path-breaker's bruised knees.(33)

In the recent explosion of south Asian postcolonial and diasporic writings in English there is scarcity of women writers from Pakistan compared to India. Increasing numbers of Indian women writers from Britain, North America, the Caribbean, East and South Africa- such as Jhumpa Lahiri, Meera Sayal, Chitra Divakaruni and Arundhati Roy-join the rank of well known writers such as Anita Desai and Bharti Mukharjee. The scarcity of women writers in English from Pakistan is inevitable because of discriminatorily gendered system of education, opportunity, modes of acculturation, and general devaluation of arts. Sidhwa was one of the first women from Pakistan to be writing fiction in English and publishing internationally now. Sidhwa and Sara Suleri are also the only two Pakistani writers to be included by Rushdi and West in their recent anthology on Indian English writers in the celebration of fifty years of independence. Some new British-Pakistani women writers beginning to publish now include Monica Alvi, Rukhsana Ahmad and Muneeza Shamsie.

Bapsi Sidhwa was born in an eminent Parsee business family of Karachi in 1939. Soon after her birth, her parents move to Lahore, where Parsis were in miniscule number, one hundred and fifty in all. The family was cut of from the mainstream of the Parsi life. She was the only child of her parents. Talking about her upbringing in Lahore, Sidhwa told Feroza Jussawalla:

> If I were brought up in Karachi, which is again very much a part of Pakistan, my experience as a child would have been totally different. I would have been brought up among the Parsis. I was brought up apart from my cousin and other relatives. My family was not a big joint family. In my home, my paternal grandmother was with us for a few years, but there was not much influence of the joint family calibre. I was largely brought up by the servants.(34)

In this age of globalization it is really very difficult to categorize some writers. Bapsi Sidhwa is one of them. She belongs to India, Pakistan and the United States, simultaneously but she likes her self to be described as "Punjabi- Pakistani-Parsi woman". She spoke to Bachi karkaria regarding her identity:

> I am Parsee first, then a Pakistani, specially a Punjabi. I'm a woman simply by gender. I don't feel American at all. My consolidated 3P identity has enriched my writing. (35)

As Sidhwa has polio she was not sent to school. She missed being with other children. She grew up in isolation. Her Anglo-Indian governess introduces her to *Little Women*, which opened up another world. She began to dwell in the fantasy within this book. Her role model was shy Victorian woman.

In the interviews Sidhwa has repeatedly said that she is first Parsee. This gives her voice a distinctive edge, and makes her one of the best known of the Zoroastrian writers today. Zoroastrian is one of the earliest religions and its origin goes back to 3000 BCE. The Zoroastrians or Parsees lived in the ancient Persia now called Iran. After the conquest of their country by the Muslim Arabs, they fled to India as religious refugees in the seventh century. Long concentrated in Bombay and other areas on the northwestern coast of the Indian subcontinent, today they are spread all over the world. In her – novels *The Crow Eaters* and *Ice-Candy-Man*, Sidhwa recounts the traditional story of the Parsis's arrival from Iran to India in the eight century, in which the Indian Prince sent his vazir to them with a full glass of milk filled to the brim signifying that his land was full and prosperous and he didn't want outsiders with a different religion and alien ways to disturb its harmony. In response, the Parsis stirred a teaspoon full of sugar carefully in to the milk and sent it back suggesting that they would get absorbed into his country like the sugar in the milk, and with their decency and industry sweeten the lives of his subjects. The Indian prince, Yadav Rana impressed by their intelligence and civilized behaviour, permitted them to live in his Kingdom on the condition that they would not eat beef, wear rawhide sandals or convert the susceptible masses.

The Zoroastrian worldview is based on the central tenet of Prophet Zoroaster's teaching. The foundation of the Zoroastrian ethical system is humata (good thought), hukta (good words) and hvarshtra (good deeds). All the social, cultural, economic, political, religious and ritualistic attitudes centrally emanate from this basic tenet of Zoroastrianism. Though Parsees enjoyed a marginal position in the Indian society during the British era, the process of Westernization never brought any change in the Zoroastrian religion. They dressed like the Europeans, smoked, drank, played cricket and pursued English education but the inner Parsee life remained unchanged. The Parsees who took lead in the process of Westernization are facing virtual extinction now, the causes of which are the decline in birth rate, high marital age, intercommunity marriages and emigration. Excessive aping of the British resulted in an uprooting of Parsee life. The greatest ironey is that the process of Westernization, brought, double alienization to Parsees. Though they were loyal to British, the British never treated the Parsees as their equal. The main problem of Parsees after the partition was – where would they go? Hindus will go to India and Muslim will go to Pakistan. As their identification with the British was total, they were alienated from the mainstream of Indian life. While giving the cause of expatriation of Parsee, V.L.V.N. Narendra Kumar has rightly pointed out:

> One of the causes of expatriation is that some prefer to work in an intellectually even more stimulating climate. The pareses prefer the West since it offers unlimited scope for growth and property. Dislocation is part of the Parsee psyche. Exiled twelve hundred years ago, they came to India. Now they are migrating west in search of greener pastures. Thus there is "double migration" in the case of Parsees. The flight in the 8th century was forced on them by Arabs where as the second is the result of a conscious and deliberate choice. (36)

The Parsees carry their ethnicity to the west –"Promised Land" (Toronto, New York, and London). Revival of interest in ethnicity, acts as a survival strategy on an alien soil, the cause of which is nostalgia. They cling to their own tradition, custom and language. Their marginality sometimes serves as spring of motivation. Very few writers like Bapsi Sidhwa, are unaffected by expatriation and remain rooted to the psyche of native land. Some writers like Bapsi Sidhwa see their native land with detachment and offer an objective image of their homeland. They acquire enough social space for themselves in the chosen land with their enterprising nature and resourcefulness. Zoroastrian religion offers them emotional space and sustains them in an alien soil.

The Zoroastrian worldview in the social sphere advocates a dynamic approach to life, leading to progress and all-rounder prosperity. The significant thing is women enjoy equal status in Parsee community. Brotherhood of man is a cardinal doctrine of Prophet Zoroaster's message. A true Parsee is always tolerant about the faiths and beliefs of others. Zorastrian worldview provides an excellent medium for adaptability and assimilation. Honesty and righteousness are notable features of Parsee life. A true Parsee is generous in charities. Parsee can survive as minority anywhere in the world because they are loyal to every ruling authority. Zoroastrianism is one of the earliest religions which preached perfect monotheism. Prophet Zoroaster raised his voice against the plurality of gods and firmly declared that the unprecedented omniscient Lord (Ahura Mazda) alone is to be adored. Zoroaster rejected ritualism and external practices of imaginary value. The value of religion is in upholding man in his life of good thoughts, good words and good deeds.

More than twelve centuries have passed but Parsee still abides their word they gave to the Indian Prince. They do not allow conversion to their faith or mixed marriages and that is the reason why their population is decreasing day by day. There are hardly a hundred thousand Parsis in the world. Bapsi Sidhwa has tried to immortalize this endangered species by capturing its quintessential ethos in her fiction. *An American Brat* and her first published novel, *The Crow Eaters* has given detailed information about the customs, ceremonies, beliefs, superstitions, rites, rituals, myths, legends and other aspects of the Parsee life. In the author's note of *The Crow Eaters,* Bapsi Sidhwa told the purpose of writing this book:

> Because of deep-rooted admiration for my diminishing community – and an enormous affection for it – this work of fiction has been a labour of love. (37)

When Sidhwa was eleven, she reads a novel *Little Women* by American novelist, Lousia May Alcott. This novel aroused her interest in reading and she realized reading could relieve her boredom. She took to reading voraciously. She read every thing that came her way – news papers, magazines and books by Indian, European, Russian and American writers, especially Raja Rao, Khushwant singh, V. S. Naipaul, Charles Dickens, P. G. Wodehouse and Tolstoy. She took her matric examination privately and got her Bachelor's degree in 1956 from Kinnaired College for women in Lahore. Talking about her early days to Sonya Dutta, Sidhwa recalls her days in Bombay, the five years of her first marriage:

> I came to Bombay like a pumpkin. My first husband said, "You cannot walk; you cannot talk; what you can do? (38)

Sidhwa lived in Bombay with her first husband, bore two children. After taking divorce she went back to Pakistan alone with her daughter but she never got the custody of her son. Her son joined her only after his father's death. Though Bombay thus left indelible scars on Bapsi Sidhwa, it also widened her horizons. She discovered the confidence of being late bloomers. She reminisces:

> Unlike Lahore where everybody knew you, in Bombay there was a wonderful anonymity, you could wear what you liked and just get on a bus. (39)

In her interview with Kazmi, she talks about the importance of Bombay in her life:

> Living in Bombay, that big city, then visiting it very frequently after my divorce, was very important to my writing. The interaction with the larger (Parsee) community really opened my eyes; the interaction with a big city opened my eyes. (40)

In 1963 she remarried Noshirwan Sidhwa, a Lahore businessman and son of a renowned freedom fighter. Twelve years senior Noshirwan was very supportive when she started writing. In 1983, Sidhwa moved to America with her husband with a view to settling there. In 1985 she was appointed Assistant Professor of the creative writing Programme at the University of Houston. In 1989 Sidhwa was Assistant professor of the MFA Graduate Programme at Columbia University, New York city, New York. From 2000-2001 she held a Postcolonial Teaching Fellowship at Southampton University, England. Though she is settled in the United States, she keeps on returning to her roots in the Indian sub-continent off and on.

Sidhwa's journey as a writer is very interesting. She told to David Montenegro, she "never thought of the writer in human terms but almost as some disembodied power that automatically produced books" (41). Sidhwa met an Afghan woman on a plane and when she told that she is a writer, Sidhwa realized that writers were made up of flesh and blood. Afghan woman asked Sidhwa to write and Sidhwa wrote just a short piece, which was published in magazine with her help. Sidhwa never look back and became one of the finest comic writers in the genre of sub continental English fiction. A turning point came in Sidhwa's life when she was invited along with her second husband to vacation in Northern Pakistan for their honeymoon. She got the story of her first novel *The Bride* here. She heard the story of a young Punjabi girl, taken across the river Indus into totally ungoverned territory to be married to a kohistani tribal. After some time the girl ran away. Her husband with his clansmen hunted her down and murdered her. When Sidhwa came back to Lahore she was so compelled to tell this story that she decided to write a short story. The short story she set out to write, turned eventually into her first novel *The Pakistani Bride,* as the nature of her experience was so intense. While writing this book she discovered her love for writing. Although she took four years to complete *The Bride*, she was so thrilled with joy that she started writing her second novel *The Crow Eaters.* She wrote secretely like Jane Austen as she was afraid she'd be laughed at. After her marriage businessmen, feudal-farmers, industrialists and professionals surrounded her social life. Only her husband knew that she was writing. She wrote about her husband's great help in her writing:

> Every thing in my life took precedence over my writing. My husband, whose reading though electric, was scant (Voltaire's *Candide,* Somerset Maugham's *Summing Up,* and Einstein's *Theory of Relativity,* were favorites), was my sounding board. I read out what I'd written and his reaction, the surprised expression that often crossed his face, the way he raised an eyebrow and sometimes looked at me, fortified me. I could trust his judgment prone on the bed, hands beneath head; he paid me tribute of attention. He rejected what he found tedious by abruptly saying so, and pointing out why – or by falling asleep. He responded to the humorous passages with glee. (42)

This is how she plunges into writing. She believed she is guided more by intuition rather than by an exercise of intellect. Writing to Sidhwa was a labour of love. In an interview to Jugnu Mohsin in Friday Times of July 26, 1989 Sidhwa admitted:

> How I abhorred those coffee parties! I tell you I would have gone mad had it not been for my writing. (43)

Reading was the only life she had. Writing became an antidote to her loneliness and boredom. Sidhwa says:

> Otherwise, my life was just restricted life of a woman with children, being a public relations officer for your husband that sort of things. (44)

Thus writing makes her life meaningful. Bapsi Sidhwa has a terrible experience when she couldn't find a publisher for her two novels. After getting many rejection slips, she decided to publish and distribute *The Crow Eaters* herself. Though *The Bride* was written earlier she decided to publish *The Crow Eaters* first because it was about her community. The experience of distributing it was very painful. She says:

> It was very frustrating to peddle your own books as I did in Lahore...I would go from bookstore to bookstore, saying, 'Please read *The Crow Eaters.* (45)

It was Jonathan Cape who gave her a break in 1980 by publishing *The Crow Eaters* in Britain. Though she got recognition after writing *The Bride, The Crow Eaters* but it was her third novel, *Ice-Candy Man* (also published as *Cracking India* in America), that made her one of the most promising English novelists from South Asia. *Cracking India* was declared a New York Times Notable Book for 1991, received the LiBeraturepries Prize in Germany. Sidhwa was awarded the Sitare-I-Imtiaz by the Government of Pakistan and the National Award for English literature by Pakistan Academy of letters in 1991. In 1992 she received the Patras Bokhari Award for Literature in Pakistan. In 1993 her fourth novel, *An American Brat* was published in America and in 1994 she received the Lila Wallace-Reader's Digest Writers' Award. Bapsi Sidhwa has daring to deal with issues of diaspora, questions of cultural identity and racial difference in *An American Brat*. Aamer Hussein has rightly pointed about this novel:

> The ambiguous, transitional nature of this work convinces me- and many other readers, I am sure – that another major work is in presently in Bapsi's imaginative laboratory. (46)

Regarding her third novel *Cracking India* what one feels – Bapsi Sidhwa's position as a writer would have been assured well into the twenty first century had she written only her third novel as it depicts contemporary world/history.

Almost all her novels are partially autobiographical. Sidhwa's growing up is partially reflected in Zaitoun's growing up in *The Bride*. The parents in the novel *The Crow Eaters* are based on her parents. Regarding *Ice-Candy Man* or *Cracking India* she says:

The first part is autobiographical, except that central character of the child is not me per se. I had to create some distance between the child Lenny and myself as a child. Otherwise I would not have been able to write freely. (47).

In *The American Brat* there are many experiences that Sidhwa and her family actually went through personally or heard about after migrating to the United States. Commenting on why she created so many American characters in *The American Brat*, she says:

> In retrospect, I am not sure it was such a good idea to attempt to create so many American characters in *The American Brat*. But I wanted to do it. I didn't want to sit in America and write only about the expatriate community I left behind. I could have done that even in Pakistan. I am having new experiences here everyday, and they need to be incorporated in fiction. There is a great dearth of candid writing about our expatriate community here and its experiences with the main stream American community. So far only Bharti Mukherjee has attempted to write on this theme. (48)

Though *The American Brat* was appreciated in Pakistan and America, some Indian reviewers have offended it. Sidhwa couldn't understand the reason:

> May be the current antagonisms between the two countries and my Pakistani origins have contributed to this hostility. I was a bit disappointed by this; because I feel myself as a part of the subcontinent. I don't feel myself 'other' from India. In fact, I have been an Indian citizen also. (49)

Sidhwa considers herself the citizen of the subcontinent rather than only as Pakistan or India. Throughout her life Sidhwa is carrying the terror and traumas of partition as she has witness it as a child. These memories emerge much later in 1988 in the form of her third novel – *The Ice-Candy Man/ Cracking India*. She wrote about partition because very little had been written about it. Partition has changed the map of the world. Its repercussions are still being felt; it's not over. We are undergoing the partition and independence movement still. Sidhwa is the witness of this partition. She has images of past which still haunts her, partition was very violent experience for all communities. Although she was very young, she saw chance killing, fires, dead bodies; Sidhwa realized there is no end to sense of hostility between the two communities. She thought:

> Over the period time the two communities would forget this hostility and heal themselves. But that has not been the case, neither in Pakistan nor in India, nor in Bangladesh. This hostility has to be dealt with. It seems that it is part of human nature to fight with somebody. If we can't fight with someone else, we fight amongst ourselves-in Pakistan for instance, the Shias and the Sunnis. This may be merely because there is not a large enough minority community to fight against. (50)

While writing about the partition Sidhwa wants to show the effect of religious hatred and violence on the people and how close evil is to the nature of man. Under normal circumstances people can be quite ordinary and harmless but once the mob mentality takes over, evil surfaces. The main theme she deals in her writing is of identity. Through her novels she tries to show how people define their identities more and more through religion. As nations people are becoming poorer and poorer. Her writing does the role of bridge building. Through her writing she shows how innocent people get involved in turmoil created by politicians.

When Sidhwa is asked whether she described herself as a postcolonial writer, she frankly told to Preeti Sing that she never understands the meaning of 'post-colonial' term. One of the questions the term "post-colonial" raises is question of English as a language. Sidhwa's diction also reflects ethnic qualities. She is conversant with several languages – English, Urdu, Gujarati and Punjabi, but she has written only in English. In an Interview to David Montenegvo, she justifies her choice of language:

> I find myself comfortable writing in this language. My written Urdu is not very good, though I speak it fluently. As for Gujarati, hardly anyone in Pakistan knows the language. In Britain, of all places, people says, "Why don't you write in your own language?" and they bear heavy political overtones to bear on this. But I think, well the English don't have a monopoly on the language of world, now. And it is a means of communicating between various

> nationalities and most immediate tool at hand. So I use it without any inhibition or problems. (51)

Bapsi Sidhwa was nurtured on Western writing in English, but as a child she did not know that the world is dominated by Western culture. In India and Pakistan many of people read *Little Women* and the works of P. G. Wodehouse and other British classics. What Sidhwa realized is that Western world does not know our culture. Sidhwa is very much conscious about Asian culture. In her interview with Preeti Sing, she tries to tell why she wants to write in English? What writer should communicate through his writing to the world where ethnicity is playing significant role. She says:

> Here we are, living in huge communities in hidden corners of world. It is time that these were seen, understood and recognized for what they are. We may be living in the other parts of world – worshipping other religions, but we also laugh, cry, and deal with similar issues, have the same notions, and live through similar turbulences. The Western world had become very callous about people from other cultures. For them we are faceless blobs. Westerners have stereotypical images about the Arabs, the Chinese, the Japanese, and the Asian etc. This becomes a way of annihilating them. And these days we do have weapons that can annihilate whole countries. This frightens me. I see injustice happening everywhere because of the hegemony of the Western world. One of the things writer can do is speak of the humanity of our people, their poverty and their naiveté… (52)

Sidhwa wanted to give a voice and a face to the people of the Third World because they are naive.

In Pakistan, a woman is constantly under pressure or scrutiny; she can't live a natural life. Politics also builds up pressure on woman. Sidhwa felt strong need to communicate her experience. She got the freedom in US – the 'land of freedom'. Regarding her diasporic experience Sidhwa says that she always felt uprooted except her stay in Mumbai, where being a Parsi among Parsis gave her a huge sense of freedom.

Displacement is a way of Parsee life. This displacement gives the necessary distance to Sidhwa as a writer. She openly talks about the pluses and minuses of US and the sub-continent. One is shocked to see her openness and daring when she talks about the policies of US. She dislikes their waste and sense of entitlement. She says for US:

> The rest of the world is discounted, disposable. The might and power they have is unprecedented, so their arrogance is untempered. They think their democracy is the best on earth, when it is deeply flawed. Corruption? The Iraq power and Halliburton are joined at the hip! They are racist, but they aren't class conscious. (53)

Sidhwa's personal experience as migrant is very good. She was warmly welcomed and helped by the local literary community – largely Jewish. She found the individual American very considerate, caring and overwhelmingly generous. Paradoxes are there in every culture, country. Paradoxically America has taught her humility and discipline. According to her Indian Diaspora are important for both cultures. After 9/11, the backlash, Muslims wanted to go back. But she tells them to stay and show that Islam is not what Americans think to be. This is the age of hyphen identity. Though people live in US for generations they are always called Asian American, Jewish-American, German-American. People are bound to identify by their food, name, and the family. Bachi Karkaria asked whether she cashed her 'exotic-eccentric' Parsee connection, she replied:

> I wish I could, but who knows of them outside? I am told, 'Look, I have trouble enough understanding you as a Pakistani or Indian, than your bring in this Zoroastrian thing. Why are you freaking one out? (54)

Thus, Bapsi Sidhwa is the most hybrid personality among all diasporic writers.

In almost all her interviews Sidhwa is asked about the sexual content in the novel. Sidhwa herself accepts that she is very shy, even timid. Journalist Anil Dharkar asks her "you look so gentle and genteel. How than you manage to write such ribald stuff?" Sidhwa replied him saying that her writing is very decent. She questions:

> If a writer writes about a boy's sexual urges it is perfectly natural; but girls also experience the same feelings, so how does that become ribald and indecent? (55)

Sidhwa is realistic and she tried to depict life as it is. Sexuality represents a very strong underlying force in everything for men, women, and children. Sidhwa has observed:

> It is not men who are promiscuous; women have these urges too. This is one of the few things that I was conscious of doing deliberately. In Pakistan, there is this enormous sexual repression on women; it is a strong undercurrent... you are not supposed to feel this or that way. You are supposed to be either good ...or a prostitute. I wanted to show that even this child, who is innocent and pure, liked people of opposite sex...that it is natural. (56)

Sidhwa has beautifully crafted this natural instinct in a gentle, funny way in her fiction.

Being a Parsee and Punjabi, humour is not away from her characters. Sidhwa has a gift for irony and humour. Sidhwa believes that there are many ways of looking at the world. Humour gives human experience a perspective and sense of balance. Commenting on the writers whose writing is only tragic, she says:

> Humour allows you to avoid what is truly tragic. I am tired of reading solemn works, especially by some writers from the subcontinent, which have been so sad that one being to feel that life is really a sorry business. I am getting a little tired of this misery, ...especially when most people writing about this are sitting very comfortably in their own lives! (57)

Parsee humour is often very ethnic and so it remains hidden from others. As day-by-day Parsee community is diminishing, they are becoming isolated. This resulted in their tendency to lose their sense of humour, and they become quite eccentric. Sidhwa tried to preserve the ethnicity and culture of Parsee community in her writing.

Sidhwa is a feminist and realist. One see in her women characters, the strength of passion, the tenderness of love, and the courage of ones convictions. As Sidhwa is in her real life, so are her women characters in her fictional world. She told Preeti Sing...how she responds to the predicament of women in society:

> I have very strong feelings about how women are treated in our part of the world. There is no doubt about his. But I would hate to sit down and rage about this in a novel. I go about it indirectly. I create characters in certain situation and let them and their circumstances reveal the issues to the reader. (58)

All her female characters are fairly beautiful, intelligent, modest but strong willed, and courageous. Rebellion is not in their nature. Their tactics vary with the nature and strength of their opponent. She has witness the partition. She listens to the cry of the women. Thousands of women were kidnapped. Terrible vendettas were enacted on their bodies to humiliate the man of other faith. Bapsi Sidhwa believes that their spirit animates all those women who have bloomed into judges, journalist, filmmakers, doctors and writers. In Bapsi Sidhwa's fiction there are multiple levels of displacement or diaspora. Her books straddle the cultures of her native Lahore, her racial 'home' Mumbai, and her present American address. She is currently editing on anthology of prose and poetry on Lahore.

In last two decades only three Indian writer's books were listed in Top Ten of New York's – Salman Rushidie's *Satanic Verses,* Arundhati Roy's *The God of Small Things*, and Chitra Banerjee's *Vine of Desire*. Recently Jhumpa Lahri's *The Namesake* is also included in it. Chitra Banerjee Divakaruni represents the current crop of writers, who are concerned with crossing over from one culture to another without compromising either, negotiating new boundaries and remaking themselves. Born in Calcutta, in 1956, the only girl in a family of four children,

Divakaruni came to US to study for a master's degree at Wright State University in Ohio, and from there went on to Berkley for Ph. D. in Renaissance literature. At that time the focus was on teaching and she taught in the Bay area for many years. Employment with Esso, an American company, fueled Divakaruni's father's curiosity about America, and thus family moves to Oklahoma. Thus corporate America played a role in author's move to America.

Divakaruni's writing came late in life and is directly tied to her migrant condition. Studying Renaissance literature and writing a dissertation on Christopher Marlowe seemed inadequate and distant from her life as a female immigrant in the United States. Divakaruni states in an interview by Joan Smith in the San Francisco Examiner Magazine:

> I think in some ways being an expatriate made me want to write because it is such a powerful and poignant experience when you live away from your original culture and this becomes home, but never quite, and then you can't go back and be quite at home there either, so you become a kind of outsider to both cultures which is hard, but very good for writers, I think to be in the position of looking in from outside observing (59)

When she received a call from India that her grandfather has passed away, Divakaruni was divested. Commenting on how she became writer and on the grief of death of her grandfather in an ancestral village of India, Divakaruni recalls:

> I was doing my Ph. D. at Berkeley at that time on a scholarship. I didn't have any money, and I couldn't go back for his funeral. It was very sad. My grandfather was very dear to me. One day soon after, I was thinking of him and I couldn't even recall his face in my mind. This frightened me. I realized how much I was forgetting about India, about my growing years, about the people I loved. I started writing...with a poem to my grandfather – as an action against that forgetting. (60)

The journey that commenced never stopped and saw a slew of novels, *The Mistress of Spices (1997)* and *Sister of My*

Heart (1999) and *The Vine of Desire (2002) Queen of Dreams (2004)*; the prize winning short story collections, *Arranged Marriage (1995)* and *The Unknown Errors of Our Lives (2001)* ; 4 acclaimed volumes of poetry – *Dark Like the River: Poems (1987), The Reasons for Nasturiums: Poems (1990), Black Candle: Poems about women from India, Pakistan, Bangladesh (1991)* and *Leaving Yuba City (1997)*. She has recently published two books for young readers, *The Conch Bearer (Aug. 2003) Neela: Victory Song (Sept. 2002)*. Some diasporic experiences described in the novels and short stories are autobiographical. In 1976, the very next day of their arrival, Divakaruni was walking down the street of Chicago with some relatives wearing a sari, then some white teenager called them "Nigger" and threw slush at them. The deeply shaming incident was never discussed, but it stayed and played in her mind and acted as the spur to kick-start her writing. Commenting on the incident she says: "Writing was a way to go beyond the silence". (61).

The "Challenges and rewards of being woman of colour in US" inspired her to question issues from a perspective she would not have had if she had not left her childhood home (62). Living in North America had also had a beneficial effect on many women writer. Divakaruni said that her mother wanted to be a writer but she could not do it because of family responsibility. Commenting on her own experience she says: "Had I lived in India I could have been expected to get married, raise and pursue a career if at all that was not very demanding. Of course women writers have succeeded in India but the struggle there is far bigger than one here" (63)

While teaching at Foothill College, she also became active in women's issues in the Bay area. She started working with Afghani women refugees and women from dysfunctional families. She realized that a lot of problems stemmed from issues of domestic violence. She has stark memories of Bangladesh refugees who fled to India to escape the massacre by the Pakistan Army in 1971. "I was then a school student", she recalls, "I would witness wasted human lives lying on railway platforms with no food and shelter. I saw how women were the victims of the Bangladesh war ". (64) The memories haunted her while teaching in an American University and in 1991; She founded an organization called "*Maitri*" that assists distressed women of South Asia. Divakaruni said:

> The work I did definitely influenced my writing. It made me think a lot more about the issues I was seeing and how it related to the lives of immigrants, and I wanted to write about it. (65)

Being a mother of two sons – it is not that much easy for Divakaruni to be a writer in US but comparatively writer's life is comfortable in America than in India. She says, "Not that one writes in order to earn money- you can't do that. Money if at all you get it, is a bonus. But every writer's sweat and blood is there in her writing, it never comes easy". (66) It is not enough for women to have room of their own to write she adds, "Unless you priorities your writing, no one else will. A man can shut himself in his room and write or read or whatever but not a woman" (67). Anjna Appachana, mother of young daughter, feels the same way. Writing her bulky novel, *Listening Now,* she feels was comparatively easier because she had more room, more space for herself in America. Divakaruni has a rigorous writing schedule which has governed her life ever since. She writes:

> My writing time is my writing time, though my children may eat micro waved burritos and I may not clean the house. (68)

At Foothill she taught every morning and then wrote in the afternoon, dropping a curtain over her cabin door so her students would know they were not to disturb her. Chitra Banerjee is a spiritual writer. Regarding home she says,

Each time we enter the house, it reminds us that we live in spiritual place, and we must make it so. (69)

As the title of her collection of short stories, *The Unknown Errors of Our Lives* hints life to her is forever mysterious – always complicated by the conflict between destiny and desire. Divakaruni once explained her reason for writing.

> There is certain spirituality, not necessarily religious, the essence of spirituality that is at the heart of the Indian Psyche that finds the divine in everything. It was important for me to start writing about my own reality and that of my community. (70)

Her approach to composition is intuitive. She begins with half an hour of meditation and sometimes even comes up with good ideas in the process. Divakaruni was judge for the 2000 National Book Awards. She says, almost shyly,

> The whole experience taught me a great deal as a writer and the writing comes from a different place, which is not a conscious part of myself – that is why I am not egoistic about it. (71)

This perspective, comes through the spiritual teaching of Gurumayi Chidvilasananda and Baba Muktananda (whose pictures she has on her writing table and whom she includes in the acknowledgements of each of her book), is what enable her to pour everything she has into the book she's working on. She says, "I think of writing as a very sacred activity. I am only the instrumental". (72) When Uma Girish asked her what does writing do for her mind and spirit? She replied:

> Writing is my great love, a great blessing in my life. It helps me to reach deep into my creativity. It calms me and gives me great joy. I thank God for it everyday. That said, my newest book always tends to be my favorite because it's my baby! I feel I've pushed myself in new directions each time. I have evolved over time and have become very interested in the multi-voiced narrative. (73)

Chitra Banerjee is very lucky star in her publishing life. Since her first book of poetry came out in 1991, she has written three books of poetry. She wrote two collections of short stories (her first collection *Arranged Marriage,* won the American Award in 1995) and novels. In addition, she also edited two anthologies on multiculturalism. Going on tour for her reading, she is pleased to see all her backlist at the bookstores. For this pleasure and her development as one of author; credit goes to the publisher Doubleday. Chitra Banerjee believes in scene. When she starts writing she begins with scene. She knows characters but she doesn't know much about it. She says, "The advantage is that the book unfold organically; the disadvantage is that I have to go back for a lot of rewriting". Her revision process is highly structured. With each book, she tries something different. "You can't hurry writing if you are going to do it," She says "otherwise, what is the point of being a writer?"(74) According Divakaruni, writing is to create art. You have to give your best attention and as much time as it takes.

One of her first memories is that of her grandfather telling her stories from *Ramayana* and *Mahabharata*. She quickly noticed," Interestingly, unlike the male heroes, the main relationships women had been with their husbands, sons; lovers or opponents. They never had any important women friend."(75). This topic would eventually become very important to Divakaruni's writing. Commenting on the need of friendship she says: "The new friendship that we make, replace the extended family and so I have really feeling the need of these friendships. I think that women friends have been so important in my own life. I wanted to write a novel celebrating that" (76) *Sister of my Heart* is the story of Anju and Sudha, from early childhood to their early twenties, began as the short story, " The Ultrasound" in *Arranged Marriage* . Her recent novel *Vine of Desire* is continuation of *Sister of My Heart* having thought over many years the nature of women's friendship and how that is really important in our lives as women and especially for immigrant women, she wrote a novel *Sister of My Heart*. Friendship among immigrant in her opinion attempt to take place of the experience of community and extended family; what she has missed the most, since leaving Calcutta at the age of 19. She expressed a concern about implications in some of the early reviews of her novel because *Sister of My Heart* is about "Women's friendship", it is quote-unquote women's novel. According to Divakaruni it is negative and harmful way to think that women should read books about women and men about men. You read about people who are different from you and that's race as well as gender.

By sharing information, contacts, endorsing worthy books by writing blurbs, attending each other readings, Divakaruni feels, - leads to the idea of writing community. Jhumpa Lahiri, whose book caries hearty endorsements from Bharti Mukharjee and Divakaruni, readily acknowledges the importance of networking. "We look out for each other and we draw strength from each other", says Divakaruni. (77) Recently in her visit to India she met Nabaneeta Dev Sen to change the notes. Late astronaut Kalpana Chawla was fan of Chitra Banerjee. In one of their meeting they spoke about their experience as women – especially as Indian women in the US and discussed the many ways they were to prove themselves in American society. It is not in sheer numbers that women writers of Indian Diaspora lead their male counterparts but they also exceed in establishing connection with women's group. Divakaruni has read for many groups including 'Sakhi' and 'Manvi' for instance. According Divakaruni networking among South Asian women's group is natural. She adds, "Many of us articulate in our books the deepest fear and trauma faced by women in India and here and show them emerge at least in many cases, as stronger and self reliant women. Some of our characters are good role models for women activists" (78). It is not only the immigrants who read the literature of Indian Diaspora, there is growing number of American who are serious about foreigners living in their middle.

Most Indian scriptures talk of the sublimation of desire as a goal but when the author encountered a new meaning in the western model where desire is positive, charged with passion and ambition and often associated with goal-getters, it fired her to explore it in *The Vine of Desire*, the sequel to *Sister of My Heart* where the protagonist Sudha falls in love with sister Anju's husband and fights the feeling with every ounce of her might. Divakaruni adds:

> I think desires are natural but we must examine them, see where they're leading us and manage them accordingly. It is when they control us that they lead to problems. Ultimately, as our scriptures indicate, one needs to rise above desire. For me this means we do the things we do out of love, and not out of need. (79)

Divakaruni explains in one of her interview with Uma Girish that she gets ideas from reading or from talking, observing people. From mysterious space of imagination also she gets the idea. She seldom watches TV. She reads all the time, in the bathroom, in bed. She is particularly interested in writing about India. Her three volumes of poetry, American Book Award winning short story collection *Arranged Marriage* and the Pen Oakland Award for fiction (*Sister of My Heart* and *The Mistress of Spices*) have established her as a major modern American writer. The characters in her book are mostly Bengali women and immigrants torn between traditional Indian ethos and modern American culture. Divakaruni's writing relates to Asian American Aesthetics as she incorporates Asian tradition in to writing such as the roles women portray through Asian history and today in society. Women are seen as people who cook, clean and follow values that are demonstrated by men. Divakaruni puts little twist on pieces of her writing. She demonstrated characters that want to break away, lead their own lives, and facilitate a sense of bravery that most women are afraid to encounter. An interesting aspect of Divakaruni's writing not only is that it reflects her personal life but that it tries to bring people together, diminish boundaries and break stereotypes of different individuals of different background, ages and variety of worlds.

She chafes when some readers – often Indians ask her if she writes with Western readers in mind who want to read either about an exotic and mythological India or about a deprived India. She offers her readers a window into the multicultural world of her characters. She adds,

> I have no particular reader in my mind but a passionate desire to tell a honest moving story. If it is good literature,

> I know, as all sensitive writers know, the reader and the writer will connect. It is inevitable. (80)

While Divakaruni explores many different richly descriptive storytelling forms, her subject remains steady. She is centrally concerned with giving shape to South Asian Women's lives in a gendered India and United States. Women form the post-colonial world face double effacement of race and gender. Their lives are shaped not only by the western hegemonic discourse but also by the patriarchal discourse. Divakaruni's writing from the postcolonial position challenges the imperial and patriarchal discourses simultaneously. Divakaruni started writing for herself. She wanted to give a way to her immigrant experience. She wanted to write about Indian women who have a great spiritual strength in spite of being the victim of racism and brutality of their men though they themselves are targets of racism in US.

She has not attended classes of creative writing and therefore the advantage of learning on one's own is that she is not influenced by any particular mode of writing or thinking. She never knew "What the 'in' fashions are in writing" (81). She has developed her own voice. She creates a voice for voiceless. She has seen problems arising out of isolation. It is important for immigrant women to interact, speak with each other. They need a listening ear like they had in India. Men also fight discrimination in the U. S. and have problems with their new roles. Divakaruni often explores issues that are central to the experience of immigration. Her rich array of characters includes Indian Americans and Indians; who have one thing in common: they are in transition and struggling for a sense of their true identity as they try to come to the terms with complex cultural and social pressures. Sarah Anne Johnson has rightly pointed out "they are lured by the forces of tradition but also drawn to the possibilities of an American future" (82)

As they reconcile the inner tension caused by the clash of two worlds, they reveal their humanity and close the perceived distance between people of different cultures.

Divakaruni wants to project this poignant experience through her characters. While reading her fiction, short stories reader feels her characters. According to Dr. Johnson, Shakespeare's characters are the genuine projeni of common humanity. As Shakespeare portrays the general not individual, Divakaruni's characters are also the representatives of immigrants in the world. It was very difficult to categorize Shakespeare's work in the forms of literature. According to Dr. Johnson, Shakespeare was true to life, nature and so he never follows the classical rules. Chitra Divakaruni also to be true to life loves to break down the boundaries between forms, such as prose and poetry, fiction and myth, fable and folklore, reality and magic. For instance, her early novel *The Mistress of Spices* is a lyrical blend of prose and poetry that shows how magic can exist in gritty urban landscapes. Commenting on Divakaruni's characters, Janice Albert says,

> Divakaruni's women are sympathetic, whole figures, decisively taking freedom in both hands, as vibrantly alive as any of Shakespeare's heroines. (83)

Truly Divakaruni has a comprehensive soul like Shakespeare. Chitra Divakaruni grew up bilingual. Her mother tongue is Bengali. She read lot of Bengali. She read lot of Bengali literature which helps her to understand – what is literature; what is done in literature; the ways in which you structure stories, poetry. As a student in India Tagore has been a great influence on her. She loved Bengali women writers like Mahasveta Devi, who has been translated into English. In Ohio, she came across Maxine Hong Kingston's *The Woman Warrior,* which had a profound effect on her thinking. Today, the roster of writers she considers most influential includes Toni Morrison, Christina Garcia, Sandra Cisneros and Louise Enid rich. In her interview with Fredric Luis Aldama, Divakaruni says:

> I try to read widely among the South Asian writers – Amitav Ghosh, Amit Chaudhary, and Rohiton Mistry – because it's as though we are all dealing with the same world, but seeing it from very different angles. Anita Desai

> has been a big influence, specially her novel *Clear Light of Day.* I learned a lot about technique and characterization from that novel particularly. (84)

Divakaruni always quotes the lines of Sylvia path and Virginia Woolf in her novel. She is influenced by Virginia Woolf's idea of a room of one's own for women. One can see the influence of Woolf in her stories where these women create their own rooms. Divakaruni admires Bharati Mukherjee for her focus on the immigrant experience. Divakaruni never believes in categories of writer....such as... feminist writer, postcolonial writer. She believes these categories are just a like circle that overlaps at certain point. She says,

> If you belong to one, you cannot belong to another. So, I am a woman writer, and I am an Asian American writer, and I am a writer of colour, and ultimately, I am just a plain writes. And if we use categories as ways of understanding, that's good but if we use them as a ways of exclusion, I think that's negative and counter productive. So I see myself as belonging to many different categories (85)

Even Amitav Ghosh and Bapsi Sidhwa never believe in these categories of writers.

REFERENCES

1. Naik M. K. "Indian English Fiction 1980-2000: Now Bcaring and Fresh Lowering", *Twentieth Century Indian English Fiction* Pencraft International 2004. p. 199.
2. Naik M. K. "Midnight's Children's Children: Thc Novel–II", *Indian English Literature 1980-2000 A Critical Survey.* 2001 p. 38.
3. Kamath A. P. "Women Writers Create a Big Impact", 1999. http://www.indianembassy.org/indus/news/media/women writting rediff p.1.
4. *Ibid.*, pp. 1-2.
5. *Ibid.*, p. 2.
6. Jairman J. N. "The study of Indian Diaspora" A Multidisciplinary Agenda" 1993 p. 5 Website: www.uohyd.ernet.in.
7. Parekh, Bhikhu "Some Reflections on the Indian Diaspora", *Journal of Contemporary Thought*, Baroda 1993 p. 105.

8. *Ibid.*, p. 106.
9. Satchidanand K. "That Third Space Interrogative the Diasporic Paradigm", *Authors, Texts, Issues, Essays on Indian Literature.* Pencraft International 2003 p. 50.
10. *Ibid.*, p. 50.
11. Sura P. Rath "Home(s) Abroad: Diasporic Identities in Third Space". *Theory and Praxis, Curriculum, Culture and English Studies* Ed. P. C. Khar, Kailash C. Baral. Sura P. Rath Pencraft International Delhi 2003 p. 96.
12. *Ibid.*, p. 97.
13. Bhabha Homi K. "Dissemination: Time, Narrative, and the Margins of the Modern Nation." *Nation and Narration.* ed. Homi Bhabha. Pub 1994, p. 291.
14. *Ibid.*, p. 292.
15. *Ibid.*, p. 300.
16. Foucault M. *Technologies of the self* ed H. Gutman et al. London: Tavistock, 1988, p. 151.
17. Bhabha Homi K. "Post Colonial Criticism", *Redrawing the Boundaries* ed. Greenblatt and Gann. Quote in Sura P. Rath, p. 82 (2003).
18. Satchidanand K., *op. cit.*, p. 51.
19. Parmeshwaran Uma, "Home is where Your Feet are, and May Your Heart Be There Too!" *Writers of the Indian Diaspora* Ed. Jasbir Jain. Rawat Publication 2003, p. 32.
20. Rushdie Salman, "Imaginary Homelands: Essays and Criticism 1981-91" *Imaginary Homelands.* Ed. Salman Rushdie. Granta Books in association with Penguin Books, India 1991, p. 213.
21. Satchidanand K. *Ibid., op cit.*, p. 53.
22. Satchidanand K. *Ibid., op cit.*, p. 55.
23. Said, Edward *Culture and Imperialism* London. Vintage 1994 p. 39.
24. *Ibid.*, p. 407.
25. *Ibid.*, p. 408.
26. Sing Gurubhagat "Expatriate Writing and Problematic Of Centre; Edward Said and Homi Bhabha" *Writers of Indian Diaspora.* Ed. Jabir Jain, p. 24.
27. Bissoondath Neil "The Uses of Ethnicity" Selling Illusion: *The Cult of Multiculturalism in Canada.* Toronto to: Penguin 1994, p. 111.

28. Rushdie Salman *op. cit.,* 1991, *p.* 221.
29. Mukherjee Bharti, "Immigrant Writing: Give us Your Maximalists." *New York Times* Books Review. p. 28.
30. Jain, Jasbir "Post-colonial Realities: Women Writing History", *Interrogative Post-colonialism: Theory, Text and Context* Ed. Harish Trivedi and Meenkshi Mukherjee Shimla: Indian Institute of Advanced Study, 1996, p. 167.
31. Sidhwa, Bapsi "Third World, Our World" *Desh Videsh. Massachusetts Review XXIX.* 4 (Winter 1988-89), pp. 703-706.
32. Chelva Kanaganayakam, "Interview with Bapsi Sidhwa" *The Toronto South Asian Review,* Vol. II No 1. Summer, 1992, p. 46.
33. Karkaria, Bachi "Ice Candy Women" Interview with Bapsi Sidhwa, 19 Feb 2005 *The Times Of India* Pune, p. 4.
34. Jussawalla, Feroza and Reed Way Da Senbrock, eds. Interview with writers of the post-colonial world. *Jackson and Londo: University Press of Mississppi* 1992.
35. Karkaria Bachi, *op. cit., Times of India,* p. 4.
36. Narandra Kumar V.L.V.N, "Westernization and Expatriation", *Parsee Novel* Prestige Books 2002, p. 14.
37. Sidhwa, Bapsi, "Author's Note" *The Crow Eaters,* Penguin Books 1980, p. 8.
38. Dutta Sonya C., "She's a Born Story Teller." Interview with Bapsi Sidhwa 6 Nov. 2005 *The Hindu,* Sunday Magazine, p. 5.
39. *Ibid., p.* 5.
40. Kazmi Laila, "Bapsi Sidhwa" Women of Pakistan 2003-2004 9 July 2004 http://www.jazbhah.org/bapsis.php
41. Dhawan R. K. and Novy Kapadia, Eds. *Novels Of Bapsi Sidhwa* New Delhi: Prestige 1996, p. 15.
42. Sidhwa Bapsi, "Why Do I Write?" *The Novels of Bapsi Sidhwa.* eds by R. K. Dhawan and Novy Kapadia. Prestige Books 1996, p. 28.
43. Dhawan R. K. and Novy Kapadia, "The Fiction of Bapsi Sidhwa", *The Novels of Bapsi Sidhwa* ed. R. K. Dhawan, Novy Kapadia Prestige Books 1996, p. 11.
44. *Ibid.,* p. 12.
45. Kazmi Laila *op. cit.,* 9 July 2004 (Same Page).
46. Hussain Aammer, "Bapsi Sidhwa, Storyteller" Introduction: The Bapsi Sidhwa Omnibus Pub. *Oxford University Press* 2001 http:/ /members.aol.com/hta/bsidhwa/revaamerhussein.html.

47. Sing Preeti, "My Place in the world" An interview with Bapsi Sidhwa. Alif: *Journal of Comparative Poetics*, No-18, Post-Colonial Discourse in South Asia 1998 *p.* 291 http://www.jstor.org/journals/cairo.html
48. *Ibid.*, p. 291.
49. *Ibid.*, p. 292.
50. *Ibid.*, p. 292.
51. Montenegrow, David, Bapsi Sidhwa: An interview *The Massachusetts Review* Winter (1990) pp. 513-533.
52. Sing Pteeti, *op. cit.*, pp. 294-295.
53. Karkaria, Bachi *op. cit.*, p. 4.
54. Karkaria, Bachi *op. cit.*, p. 4.
55. Dutta Sonya *op. cit.*, p. 5.
56. Rajan Julia, "Cracking India" In Interview with Bapsi Sidhwa. http://monsoonmag.com/interview/13intersidhwa.html p. 6.
57. Sing Preeti *op. cit.*, p. 297.
58. Sing Preeti *op. cit.*, p. 298.
59. Brunda Moka Dias, Biography, Chitra Banerjee Divakaruni. Book Title: *Asian American Novelists: A Biographical Critical Sourcebook* ed. By Emmanuel S. Nelson. Pub. Greenwoog Press, West-Port 2000, p. 87.
60. Uma Girish, Straddling Two Cultures, California Literary Review. Chitra Banerjee Divakaruni Interview http://www.calitreview.com/interviews/int.divakaruni8002.htm, p. 2.
61. *Ibid.*, p. 1.
62. Sethi R. C., "They Forgive My Fiction" http://www.ittelindia.com/achal/archivelapanaa/fiction p. 1.
63. Kamath A. P. *op. cit.*, p. 3.
64. *The Week* (Magazine, India), March 2003, p. 34.
65. Banerjee Neela, "Mistress of Self" http://www.asianweek.com/20010040/ael/chitradivakaruni.html p. 2
66. Kamath A. P. *op. cit.*, p. 3.
67. Kamath A. P. *op. cit.*, p. 3.
68. Farmanfarmaian Roxane, "Chitra Banerjee: Writing from Different Place", *Publisher's Weekly* NewYork: May 14,2001 vol. 248, p. 46
69. *Ibid.*, p. 47.
70. Biography-Criticism Chitra Banerjee Divakaruni. http://voices.cla.umn.edu/authors/chitradivakaruni.html

71. Farmanfarmaian Roxane, *op. cit.*, p. 47
72. Farmanfarmaian Roxane, p. 47
73. Uma Girish *op. cit.*, p. 3
74. Farmanfarmaian Roxane, *op. cit.*, p. 46
75. Biography Criticism http://voice.cla.umn.edu/authors/chitradivakaruni.html
76. (Sethi R. C. *op. cit., p.* 2) Kamath A. P *op. cit.*, p. 4.
77. Kamath A. P *op. cit.*, p. 4.
78. Kamath A. P *op. cit.*, p. 2.
79. Uma Girish *op. cit.*, p. 3.
80. Profile by Arthurs J. Pais. Feb 1999. http://www.saja.orj/divakaruni.html, p. 1
81. Fredrick L .A. "Unbraiding Tradition, An Interview with Chitra Divakaruni" *Journal of South Asian Literature* vol. 35 Number 142(2003) p. 3
82. Jonhnson R. A., "Writing Outside the Lines". *The Writer*. Boston: March 2004, Vol. 117, p. 20.
83. Janic Albert, "How Now, My Metal of India?" *English Journal Urbana*: Sept. 1997, Vol. 86, p. 99.
84. Fredrick L. A., *op. cit.*, p. 4
85. Fredrick L. A., *op. cit.*, p. 5

Chapter 2

Nationalism, Transnationalism, Liminality

Diasporic Experience in Bapsi Sidhwa

Nationalism, Transnationalism, Liminality: Diasporic Experience in Bapsi Sidhwa

Parsee novel in English came into its own in the Eighties with the appearance of Bapsi Sidhwa-on the literary scene. Bapsi Sidhwa is Pakistan's leading diasporic writer. Her novels deal with the themes and issues related to contemporary Parsee life, which is in a state of transition. The distinctive ethnicity of Parsee life is depicted exhaustively in her works. Her novels deal with the question of dislocation, the quest for an identity in an alien land. Her novels reflect her personal experience of the Indian Subcontinent's Partition, abuse against women, immigration to the US and membership in the Paris/Zoroastrian community. The emergence of promising Parsee writers like Rohiten Mistry, Firdaus Kanga, Boman Desai, Farrukh Dhondy and Ardashir Vakil have given a new direction to Parsee novel in English. These entire novelists live in abroad. Hence when we deal with the fiction written by Parsis, we are talking mainly about expatriate writers.

Writing about how dislocation is part of the Parsee psyche and what did Parsee novels deal with, Keki N. Daruwala writes:

> So for much of Parsi writing has been about memory and in their context memory and identity often get merged into each other. Parsis preserved their heritage, their

> scriptures, a part of their culture all these 1300 years. They still remember the Diaspora from Iran. Hence memory is heritage. Memory is identity. Once the stocks of historic/ mythical incident have been exhausted, they will need to look ahead rather than look back. [1]

There are different patterns of migration. Parsee Diaspora is always benefited by migration. Cicely Havely has compared Parsee Diaspora with other Diaspora. He Writes:

> Unlike the Jews and the Chinese, the Parsi Diaspora yearns for neither a spiritual nor a familial homeland, and their allegiances are place of settlement. Thus it is possible for migration to be a subject of comedy to such a relaxed and cosmopolitan community in total and poignant contrast with the reactions and fate of the Muslim villagers who have misfortune to live just miles closer to Amritsar than Lahore. For them prospect of migration is almost literally unthinkable. [2]

In Bapsi Sidhwa's fiction, there are multiple levels of displacement or dispora, though within the subcontinent-from central India to Lahore in *The Crow Eaters*, from Lahore to Amritsar in *Ice-Candy Man* (the migration shared by millions). In 1947 her country changed under her from India to Pakistan. Her migration from Lahore to New York in *An American Brat* is for creative reason. Dislocation and Diaspora are the creative thrust of her fiction in which history is the compelling factor. Bapsi Sidhwa has enjoyed benefits of hybridization before leaving home to US, being the daughter of an urbane Parsi family. Commenting on the pattern of migration in Bapsi Sidhwa's Novels, Cicely Havely remarks:

> In Sidhwa's work, there is no migration or Partition without loss. Even Freddy's jovial rise exerts its price. But the prevalent comedy of her work also suggests that migration is one of life's essential rhythms and that the losses it incurs are made good with gains in Self-Knowledge. [3]

Thus hybridity helps Bapsi Sidhwa to develop her maturity. For many writers, their multi-cultural situation' has become the 'modes of perception' which Meenakshi Mukherjee anticipated [4] and asset rather than loss. In all Sidhwa's novels hybridity of migrant is a cause for celebration, not regret.

Sidhwa has written four novels to date. These are *The Crow Eaters* (1980), *The Pakistani Bride* (1982), *Ice-Candy Man* (1988)-published as *Cracking India* in the USA- and *An American Brat* (1993). Her first three novels are set in Pakistan and the fourth novel moves back and fourth between Pakistan and the United States. Being a Parsee Zoroastrian, She belongs to a minority etno-relogious group in a Pakistan, which is becoming more Islamic-almost fundamentalist day by day in their socio-political life. Born during the final gaps of the Raj, Sidhwa spent her early years in India; than she found her larger community changed in Pakistan, a nation created in Partition. Her native city Lahore was transformed overnight, when millions were uprooted, their lives often destroyed, sometime rebuilt, some lived out in anguish. As a child she witnessed great historical moments: the combined apprehension and elation over Independence followed by the bloodshed of partition, the chaotic time of resettling refugees.

After the partition Parsees in Pakistan were under the impact of Muslim culture. In the early sixties Parsee ladies were using clothes according to their culture but in the seventies Parsee girls were unable to wear frocks and sleeveless blouse. Nilufer E. Bharucha has explained about the status of Parsee community after Partition:

> Parsees had in general feared decolonization but did not really suffer in the aftermath of the end of Empire. In India the pioneering Parsee Nationalists had created a fund of goodwill, which postcolonial Parsees could draw upon. In Pakistan, riots stood them in good stead. Here Parsee became a respected minority community. However the increasing Islamization of the body politics of Pakistan has had an impact on most Parses, especially the women, who have had to toe the official line on dress code and other women related laws. [5]

Parsee women were threatened by the increasing encroachment by fundamentalist – Islam on their ethenic space. *An American Brat* depicts this problem, which forced Zareen Ginwalla to send her daughter Feroza to USA. The time depicted in the novel is the late seventies. Zulfikar Ali Bhulto is in Jail and Islamic fundamentalism is growing in Pakistan. The heroine of the novel, Feroza, a sixteen- years-old girl has been carefully brought up in the small, Prosperous Parsee Community in Lahore. Her parents want to save her from the impact of further influence of Muslim government. Feroza was becoming more and more backward day by day. She is confused with Parsee culture at home and Muslim culture outside the home. Zareen was shocked when Feroza objects to her wearing a modern dress:

> I went to bring Feroza from school today. I was chatting with Mother superior on the veranda- she was out enjoying the sun- and I had removed my cardigan. Feroza pretended she didn't know me.
>
> In the car she said: 'Mummy, please don't come to school dressed like that'. She objected to my sleeveless sari-blouse! Really, this narrow-minded attitude touted by General Zia is infecting her, too. I told her: 'look, we are Parsee, everybody knows we dress differently. [AB, P.10]

Zareen realized that thing has changed in Pakistan, the claustrophobic atmosphere of Zia's islamization is dangerous to Parsee community:

> Could you imagine Feroza cycling to school now? She'd be a freak! Those *gundaas* would make vulgar noises and bump into her and *mullahs* would tell her to cover her head. Instead of moving forward, we are moving backward. What I would do in '59 and '60, my daughter can't do in 1978! Our Parsee children in Lahore won't know how to mix with Parsee kids in Karachi or Bombay. (AB P.11)

Feroza was fed up of hot political discussion at home. Zareen was from Bhutto's side. She "was really hopeful when

Bhutto was elected. For the first time I felt it didn't matter that I was not a Muslim or that I was a women."(AB P.11)

Though Bhutto was open-minded, after coming in the power nothing was changed. He invited the Martial law. As Cyrus, Zareen's husband pointed out to his wife:" Your Bhutto also let us down, asking the army to control law and order! Didn't he know he was inviting Martial law? Nationalizing even the cotton gins, ruining the economy"(AB P.11)

Zareen decided to send Feroza to the USA during the summer vacation, where her brother Manek, a graduate student at M.I.T., can look after her. She feels, "Travel will broaden her outlook, get this puritanical rubbish out of her head."(AB P.14) Khutlibai, Zareen's mother tried to appose this proposal but Cyrus accepts it because he remembers how timidly Feroza had behaved with a young boy in their drawing room who came to ask her-whether she will enact in college annual gathering. Feroza was happy and excited when her trip to the USA was finalized.

This novel chronicles earlier novel *The Crow Eaters*. Faredoon Junglwala and Putlibai are the great grandfather and mother of Zareen. *An American Brat* is a result of Sidhwa's years of living in the United State and tells of the problems of adjustment to a new culture as experienced by her heroine Feroza who comes to visit and then to study in the U.S. and who becomes "an American brat", according to some of he relatives. Talking about the theme of *An American Brat* to Naila Hussain, Bapsi Sidhwa says that:

> Naturally, the book deals with the subject of the 'cultural shock' young people from the subcontinent have to contend with when they choose to study abroad. It also delineates the clashes, the divergent cultures generate between the families 'back home' and transgressing progeny bravely groping their way in the New World. (P.6)

The theme of immigrant is quite prominent in this novel. The issue of cultural difference moves from periphery to center in this novel. *An American Brat* deals with the intercultural theme, which has assumed vital significance for many a postcolonial novelist. Several writers from one-time British colonies have treated this theme, including the Hong-Kong born novelist Timothy Mo in *Sour Sweet* (1982), Bharthi Mukharjee in *Jasmine* (1989). Earlier Anita Desai explored this theme in *Bye-Bye Blackbird* (1971), recently, the Indian born writer Chitra Banerjee Divakaruni in *Arranged Marriage* (1995), Jhumpa Lahiri in *The Namesake* (2004). As people move from one part of the world to another seeming to dissolve national boundaries, the formation and maintenance of community take on new dimensions, as community becomes more fluid. *An American Brat* is a significant contribution to the literature of Diaspora.

Discussing the major trends in postcolonial literatures, Ashcroft, Griffiths and Tiffin write:

> A major feature of postcolonial literatures is the concern with place and displacement. It is here that the special postcolonial crisis of identity comes into being, the concern with the development of recovery of an effective identifying relationship between self and place. (7)

In Feroza's case also when she came to U.S.A, she felt uprooted; her sense of self is eroded by displacement. The sudden swing from conservative milieu of Lahore to the exhilarating 'surreal world' of New York disorients her. During the course of the story, Sidhawa touches upon almost all aspects of the new immigrants and visitors experiences in the United States at first hand. Some of the incidents are funny some are ugly and painful.

Feroza was highly delighted at the news of her departure to U.S.A. She repeats herself,

> "I'm going to America, I am going to America!" America means to her at the moment "the land of glossy magazines, of 'Bewitched' and 'Star Trek', of rock stars and jeans...(AB, P.27)

She was very much eager and excited to go to America. At the airport, everyone in the family gave her instruction.

She is told that she shouldn't talk to the strangers and accept anything to eat and drink, as it might be drugged. Feroza followed all the instructions given to her. She herself has also prayed to Ahura Mazda for her long and safe journey to their fire temple:

> Come to my help, O Ahura Mazda! Give me victory, power and the joy of life. (AB, P.42)

The moment the plane lands at Kennedy airport, Feroza is triumphant and glowing. She is dazzled by the orderly traffic of rushing people, the bright lights and warmed air, the extraordinary cleanliness and sheen on floors and furnishing, and the audacious immensity of the glass and steal enclosed spaces.

The ruthless interrogation of custom officer realizes her for the first time that she is in a strange country amidst stranger. There is a moment of confusion as her Pakistani passport opens from the wrong end. Unlike English, Urdu was written from right to left and not vice versa. Feroza is subjected to a rather inhumane treatment by custom officer. He asked her a number of questions – what was her name, how long she would stay, where she would stay, how old was her uncle, what did he do, was he a US citizen, resident or visitor. As Feroza was confused, innocent, emotional, her answers do not seem satisfactory and she was directed to secondary inspection-after collecting her luggage.

After crossing the hurdle of the custom officer, she tries to cope the different life-style of the Americans and the modern technology used by them. She is unfamiliar with the moving staircase, the escalator, which, one finds in abundance in the small store in America. She has good experience also. An elderly couple helps her to cross this hurdle. The next problem Feroza faces is of carrying her outsized suitcases. She finds Young men coming and taking away carts one by one after inserting a dollar bill in a slot. The other Young man shows her how to insert a dollar bill and get a cart. She realizes that the people around her were busy; none of them had even bothered to glance her way or stare at her, as they would have in Pakistan. She has first taste of freedom:

> She knew no one, and no one knew her! It was a heady feeling to be suddenly so free-for the moment, at least-of the thousand constraints that governed her life. (AB, P.58)

As soon as Feroza saw her uncle, she steers her cart towards him. A woman in black uniform stops her: "Hey, you can't leave the terminal. Your passport, please"(AB, P.59). She was directed to secondary inspection. Feroza was so nervous that answer does not reach the inspector who gets impatient and feels irritated at her response. Feroza falls into their trap when she blurts out that her uncle is a student and he also works at two other jobs to make extra money. Evidently, she does not know that it is a crime for foreign students to work. She is told that her uncle would haul before an immigration judge and most likely deported. Manek, her uncle some how tried to convince custom officer regarding the charge of working at two different jobs:

> I work in the university cafeteria and at other odd jobs there, officer. She's just arrived, she doesn't know. I receive enough money from home for my tuitions and living expenses. I can show you my bank drafts and statements to prove it. I can get a letter from my University. I work only for them. I'm permitted that. (AB P.63)

The custom officer accuses Feroza that she is a liar- she has no uncle in America and her so-called uncle is actually her fiance. Her ears couldn't believe and she started crying. The custom officer starts inspecting each and every item in her bags- the shoes, the toiletries, the underwear, a sanitary pad. Feroza couldn't bear this humiliation and loses her patience. She snatches the nightgown from him and says, "To hell with you and your damn country. I'll go back!"(AB, P.64)

The inspector realizes he has exceeded his powers and leaves the place. Manek assures him that girl will go back at the end of three months or whenever her visa expires and he will send a copy of his passport and visa and a letter from his University certifying that he doesn't work anywhere else.

The officers allow them to leave the airport. In this way her encounter with the custom officer was over and she left the airport.

Expatriation is a complex phenomenon, which involves a transition from the known to the unknown. It is shift from a familiar set of values and relationships at home to an alien value system and relationship in the chosen land. Viney kirpal writes about the dilemma of the expatriate writer:

> He is not the de-regionalized, de-racinated man of the modern west. His marginality itself is the result of his race, region and history. And he writes with this realization in his bones. (8)

Regarding Parsi ethnicity, and their assimilation in alien land and writers like Sidhwa,, V.L.V.N. Narendrakumar observes:

> The Parsees carry their ethnicity to the "Promised Land" (Toronto, London or New York). Their marginality sometime serves as spring of motivation. Some writers, like Bapsi Sidhwa, are unaffected by expatriation. They remain rooted to the psyche of native land. In the twentieth century, the creative epicenter shifted from the center to the margins. The Post-colonial writers are, in the words of Rushdie, 'Writing back to the center (9)

Through the close analysis of the novel *An American Brat,* it becomes obvious that Parsee ethnicity has helped Feroza to adjust in U.S.A. and face the challenges of the new world. Sidhwa chronicles not only the glitz and glamour but also the ugliness and squalor of the USA. After leaving the Kennedy airport, Manek tries to cool Feroza:

> You will love New York. I've planned it so we can spend a week here. Then we'll get back to Cambridge. If I get the time, we'll even go to Disneyland.(AB P.66)

Feroza was excited to see the garlands of lights outlining the iron rhythm of the bridge they are racing along, the sumptuous red tail-lights of the cars ahead. The incredible lights, ships in an incredible river excite Feroza so much that she utters in Punjabi: "Vekh! Vekh! Sher-di-bation!" (AB, P.67)

Feroza's initiation, both her innocence and amazement reflect the cultural shock of the migrants during their initial trip from the third world to the first world. The next day Feroza's tour of New York starts. Her uncle Manek and Feroza ride the ferry to the Statue of Liberty and explore the iron innards of the stern figure presiding over the ocean. They stroll with nannies and babies through zoo at Central Park. The opulence and shopping in New York simply mesmerize Feroza. She moves amidst the dazzling wares, bewitched by displays of merchandise, which attract her with a suction-like force. Later she insists on window-shopping on Fifth Avenue. When they have lunch at McDonald's, Feroza is wondered at the quick service and the quantities of fries, ketchup, and the ice in the coke. The America and Americans she encounters enchant her. This sudden shift from Lahore to New York has placed Feroza in next century.

While presenting glamour and efficiency of the America, Sidhwa also depicts the unpleasant and violent aspect of the life in post-industrial, consumerist and technology-dominated society. Her uncle also shows her the other side of New York, "the lookouts, runners, drug dealers, elegant transvestites, male prostitutes and hubs of poverty" (AB, P.80) Feroza was shocked to see the port Authority of bus terminal, in which the homeless and discarded, "ragged and filthy men and women were spreading scores of flattened cardboard boxes to sleep on in the bus terminal."(AB, P.80) Feroza was used to poverty and ugliness-sweat, urine, open drains in Pakistan but she couldn't accept poverty and the smell of filth in the first world. She was about to omit:

> This was an alien filth, a compost reeking of vomit and alcoholic belches, of neglected old age and sickness, of drugged exhalations and the malodorus ferment of other substances she could not decipher. The smell disturbs her psyche; it seemed to her they personified the callous heart of the rich country that allowed such savage neglect to occur. The fetid smell made her want to throw up. She

ran out of the building, and, leaning against the wall of the terminal, began to retch. (AB, P.81)

Feroza realizes that "America is not all Saks and skyscrapers."(AB P.81) Feroza has another unpleasant and horrible experience when she confronts a sex maniac at the YMCA bathroom. Already Feroza was feeling uncomfortable while using the facilities in women's bathroom and when she raises her head to look into the mirror she saw a man's bloodshot eyes are staring at her, hideously examining her not as a woman but as a specimen of the female gender. As she whirls around, the man's face suddenly breaks into a cunning, lewd, brown-toothed grin and he says:" How Ya doing, baby? Ya wanna poke?"(AB, P.70) Feroza tried to run away from the place but another man moved to block her path and he says: "Howja like it if I rub it up against ya?" Feroza took several wrong turns and somehow located her room. The next day Manek went as a guard along with her to bathroom.

The visitors from the third world countries are surprised to see the amount of crime in this affluent country. New immigrants are often warmed by well-meaning women, friends about how careful they should be on streets and parking lots otherwise they would be raped and robbed. This everyday crime is not that much common in the third world country. Sidhwa has written about the most horryfiying American experience with Feroza. One afternoon, while taking the elevator up to the YMCA where she is staying with Manek, Feroza gets off at the wrong floor; she steps out, not knowing what to do. A sympathetic soul asks her to go down again, get into the correct line, and then take the elevator that goes to the fifteenth floor, the numbers being marked on the top. Following the advice of seemingly well-meaning women, Feroza takes the fire stairs. Once on the stairs, however, Feroza finds herself in a very different world from bright shopping centers where Manek had taken her. She becomes disoriented and panic-stricken. The air is rank, smelling of stale, cigarette smoke, urine and decaying refuse. It is cold and dark. An unsetting weakness creeps into her legs. She tries the doors on different floors but all of these are locked. She shouts for help but no one listen. She prays to God but it does not help. She imagines someone is following her:

> America assumed a ruthless, hollow cylindrical shape without beginning or end, without sunlight; an unfathomable concrete tube inhabited by her fear. She was sure something monstrous was crouched in the impervious shadows that patrolled this alien-domain· ferocious sewer rats, brutish Doberman-breathing softly, waiting patiently. (AB, P.90)

With fear that somebody is coming up she started banging with the palms of her hands, she screams: "Open the door for God's sake, open the door! Can't anybody hear me? Please somebody..."(AB, P.92). A Japanese man who, hearing her terrified scream opens the fire escape door and finally rescues her. The man scolds her for being a fool: "Never do that ...never! You could be murdered. No one would know. All kind of shitty people...drugs!"(AB, P.94). Sidhwa shows-how innocent and careless third world women are, as they are overprotected in their country. They have no practical knowledge. The Japanese scolded Feroza on her foolishness:

Who is this woman? Show her to me! Right now you could be raped! You must have your head examined .....You're not a baby. You got no business in New York it got no sense."(AB,P.94).

In spite of these hostile, horrible experiences Feroza decided to live in America to make her career and to become independent woman. Her encounter with the culture of chosen land results in her symbolic rebirth. Her ethnic anxiety triggers off her quest for identity in the alien land. Towards the end of the narrative her process of assimilation is complete. According Viney Kirpal, an exile rarely returns home:

> On the one pretext or the other, he continues to stay on. The rejection he experiences in the white man's land hurts no doubt, but there is hope and a fierce inexplicable will to go on, to succeed. (10)

Even Edit Villareal suggests in a review that the coming-of-age theme is closely linked with the theme of immigration in Bapsi Sidha's novel:

> Coming of age is never easy. Coming of age as a woman is even harder. But coming of age as a female immigrant in a foreign country may be the most difficult of all. For any women born into societies with restrictive social and political codes, however, immigration may be the only real way to come of age.(11)

Feroza, after getting a crash course from Manek about how to survive in the states is soon on her way. She decides upon a college in Twin Falls, Idaho. Manek is happy because it is in Mormon territory. There is the ban on linquor, striptease, and prostitution. And in most restaurants even coffee is not served. Here she will not be exposed to free and easy ways of the rest of America. Here she finds the joys and tribulations of American campus life. Her American roommate Jo helps her in assimilation to American lifestyle. She acts, talks and dresses like an American girl. The shy and conservative Feroza turns into a confident and self-assertive girl. She learns to drive, drink, dance and use the American slang. She says: " may-nayze" and "gimme", (AB, P.154) she uses expletives like "motha-fuka" (AB, P.154) and "shit" and "ass-hole"(AB, P. 159). Jo picks up men casually but Feroza is still restrained. Feroza knows that her parent would be surprised at her changed lifestyle but she thinks of this behavior as a form of initiation:

> At the same time, she felt she was being initiated into same esoteric rites that governed the astonishingly independent and unsupervised lives of young people in America. Often as she sat among them, Feroza though she had taken a phenomenal leap in perceiving the world from a wider, bolder, and happier angle." (AB, P.164)

The timid, shy Feroza even commits the cardinal sin of smoking-to Parsis fire is the symbol of Ahura Mazda (God) and smoking an act of desecration. She flirts with an Indian student Shashi at the University of Denver where she studies hotel management. Later, she has a tempestuous love affair with a handsome young American Jew David Press.

To highlight the change in Feroza, Sidhwa uses the differences in US and Pakistani cultures. Sidhwa has a keen eye for the differences in the life style of Americans and Pakistanis. These differences are also conveyed through her genuine Parsee humor. One lesson that Asians learn is that of personal hygiene. While Asians bathe, use soap and perhaps talcum powder if they can offer it – few use deodorants. While moving around in Bloomingdale's on Lexington Avenue, Manek announces with profound certitude:

> I can smell a desi!....I bet there's an Indian or Pakistani in the room. One can smell a native from a mile.(AB P. 73)

After carefully scouting the area with his nose, like a hound on a promising trail, he returns to the spot from where he started and realizes that it is no other than Feroza. He says, "You're the smelly desi!"(AB P.74) However she can't smell her own smell. Manek says, "You can't smell your own smell, stupid, people are going to start fainting any minute." (AB, P.74) Feroza tried to convince about the smell, "It's this dammed nylon-stain kamiz" Feroza honestly accept the fact." It starts smelling if it becomes hot. I can't help it. As if you never sweat!" (AB P.74) Manek got irritated:

> "That's the trouble with you desis. You don't even know what a deodorant is, and you want to make an atom bomb!" (AB, P.74)

Bharti Mukharjee in her short story, "A wife story", also narrates how people are changed in America, if in nothing else, at least in the use of deodorants and fragrances. Feroza's uncle, in his crash course also taught her how she must rub on deodorants to have an odour-free armpit. Manek also taught her how to exploit the American system in various ways. He takes her to restaurant in Boston. He orders T-bone steaks. He asked her to leave a portion uneaten. He himself leaves the reddish stump in the center of his steak uneaten. He than complaint Feroza's steak is burnt and his raw. The manager sees through Manek's game and orders him to get out. Feroza follows Manek out and feels humiliated. Manek tells her that she must learn to be humble in life because it is pride that causes the sense of humiliation.

Manek teaches her to be less trusting and more alert. He also told her to listen others and never interrupt. American people never like interruption. He shows her how to open the plastic wrappers without tearing at them with teeth. Whenever he sees her wrestling with jar or juice bottle or tamperproof vial, he says,

> Remember this: If you have to struggle to open something in America, you're doing it wrong. They have made everything easy (AB P.140)

Feroza's American education was not a one-way transaction. If Feroza learned to live independently in the USA, she too changed lives in return. She brought lot of changes in Jo. Feroza discovered that Jo was naive; she believed everything anybody told her. In America though it is good sign that children lives independently but when her boyfriend cheated Jo, she cried.... She was almost desperate. Though Americans love "individuality", they are "lonely", there is no one to share their sorrow or happiness. In Asian countries children are over protected. Parent's overprotection becomes interference in their children's life. She finds American way of upbringing entirely different:

> And, surprisingly, even though Feroza found the Miller's way of life admirably tolerant and eminently desirable, she could not imagine it transposed to any community, whether it was Christian, Muslim, Hindu, Sikh, or Parsee, in her part of the world. What would life be like in her family and in Lahore without the extravagant guidance and dire warnings, the endless quoting of homilies, and the benign and sometimes not so benign advice, inquisitiveness and interference? (AB, P.209)

Feroza gave moral support to Jo. Jo believed whatever she saw on T.V. As a member of a totalizing society, where media was controlled by the state, Feroza had "learned from her parents, servants, friends and relatives, to question the news, form an opinion only after she had absorbed through word of mouth and the rumour mill other opinions" (AB P.170) Like most postcolonial, Feroza was politically aware for:

> In Pakistan, politics concerned everyone – from the street sweeper to the business tycoon- because it personally affected everyone, particularly women, determining how they should dress...how they should conduct themselves in the four walls of their homes. (AB P.171)

Nilufer Bharucha observes:

> Her keen sensibility soon detected the bias in the first world's reporting of news about Pakistan and other Third world countries (12)

Feroza's guidance taught Jo to became aware of, " the extent of the bias and how pervasive it was on all the networks." (AB, P.171) T.V. make Feroza aware of "disturbing insights in American's foreign policy, into the nature of the fissure that existed at the core of America's political heart, which like divine Zurvan's mythic face, was divided into darkness and light". (AB P172)

Though diasporic experience constitutes the core of narrative in *An American Brat* Sidhwa interweaves a commentary on Pakistani politics, an exposition of Parsee community and religious rites, mixed marriages, operation of women and the marginalization. Thus her literary canvas is much broader than Bharti Mukharjee's canvas. Though she deals with several themes but above all, this novel examines a very contentious and controversial issue amongst the Parsee community, the tradition of prohibition of marriage to a non-Parsee. The Parsee, a minority culture group anywhere in the world, have tradition of not allowing either conversion and expelling those who marry outside community. Sidhwa wants to highlight that the repercussion of this tradition is linked to survival of the community.

Sidhwa shows the paradox in Manek's attitude towards women though he is living in America. Manek is the symbol of patriarchy. Manek enjoys the company of liberated women but when it comes to marriage, he turns to Lahore in vacation and agrees to an arranged marriage. He finally chooses a velvet-eyed, fair-skinned girl Aban to whom 'divorce' is an 'ill omened word'. (AB, P.258). Such a choice reflects the Parsee psyche and a curious paradoxical attitude towards women. Westernized education for Parsee women is welcomed, yet female behaviour is codified and attempts are made to curtail any form of self-assertion.

In depicting the Americanization of Feroza, Sidhwa contrasts the confined atmosphere of girl's lives in the subcontinent with the liberated atmosphere they enjoy in the states:

> Feroza had grown up, like most girls in the sub continent, believing that everything she expected of life would be hers after marriage. The denial of her most insignificant wish was followed by comments like. "You'll reign like a queen in your husband's house. You can do as you wish once you're married. (AB, P.219)

Feroza decides to spend her winter vacation in Lahore. She was warmly welcomed by her family and she noticed the changes in the family and the country. Her grandmothers look older than before. People have forgotten Bhutto and his martyrdom. Secularism has given way to Islamic foundation. Non-Muslims are eyed with suspicion. The Islamic laws are governing the law courts. The gender bias and poverty both are increasing. Feroza finds herself misfitted in her own home country where she once fitted comfortably. When her mother talked about her marriage, the confident Feroza rejected the possibility of getting married; as she wanted do her career first and than marriage. But to please her mother and grandmother she says:

> I refuse to die an old maid! It's only a matter of few months, a year at most. When I'm back I'll have a good look at all boys, and I'll marry the handsomest!" (AB, P.240)

Zareen was shocked by the change in her daughter when Feroza makes her realize:

> You've never worked, Mum, You don't know how thrilling it is to earn your own money. And spend it. (AB, P.240)

> Zareen would see that her daughter had "a sense of control over her life, a sense of accomplishment that Zareen had very little experience of". (AB, P.240).

After returning back to America Feroza fell in love with a young American Jew David Press, who was big, blond and blue-eyed. She soon moved in to the house he shares with others and their physical intimacies became more intense. It was as good as living together. Feroza was feeling guilty – she wonders if she is the same girl who lived in Lahore and went to the convent of the Sacred Heart. She decides to seek permission from her parents to marry David and sends a letter along with his photograph to her mother. Not only Zareen but the entire family was shattered because they know the repercussions of marrying Non-Parsee. The family and close friends had a urgent meeting,

> For the subject was much larger than just Feroza's Marriage to an American. Mixed marriages concerned the entire Parsee community and affected its very survival: God knew, they were few enough....Parsees were a gravely endangered species" (AB,P.268)

Zareen went to America to bring her "brat" back to her senses.

Zareen was excited with new world – like a young girl, she was enjoying shopping, eating. She was influenced by the air of freedom and in spite of the regular homilies she delivered to her daughter on the subject of 'mixed marriage', she began to like Feroza's young man and "wished that David was a Parsee-or that the Zoroastrians would permit selective conversion to her faith" (AB,P.287) Zareen recalls Bunny's protest and thinks that teenagers in Lahore were right. The various Anjumans must introduce minor reforms if they wish their tiny community to survive. Zareen questions the gender bias in her religion which allowed " a Parsee man who married a "non" to retain his faith when a Parsee women couldn't". (AB, P.287) She wonders the Parsi ban on conversions-

> How could a religion whose prophet urged his followers to spread the Truth of his message in the holy Ganthas- the songs of Zarthustra- prohibit conversion?" (AB, P.287)

Zareen's other mind reminds her if Feroza marries David, it would be the end of the world. Her daughter would be cut off from culture. Zareen's anxiety as mother is genuine. The state of ambivalence is the core of the cultural difference. As a mother she cannot see the sorrow on the face of Feroza. Some how by telling Parsee rituals of marriage, she managed to keep David away from Feroza. It finally becomes clear to him that Feroza's culture is entirely different from his and he cannot adjust himself to it:

> He felt inadequate, wondering if we could cope with some of the rituals and behavior that, despite his tolerant and accepting liberality, seemed bizarre. Stuff his mouth with sweets break a coconut on his head! And, were he by some gross mischance accepted to the Zoroastrian faith, which fortunately was not permissible, he'd have the singular honor of having his remains devoured by vultures and crows in a ghastly Tower of Silence. (AB, P.309)

The ethno-religious pressures, she applied finally broke David and "She had knocked him out with sugar" as the old Parsee proverb went. Luckily he gets a job with a firm in California and he leaves Deniver. Zareen goes back to Lahore. Feroza feels shocked, insecured and uprooted for sometime but she soon bounces back. She sought refuge in her own ethnic identity:

> Feroza dug out her *sudra* and *kusti*. They had been hibernating for a long time...(invoked) Ahura Mazda's blessings..... All at once the image at the holy *atash* in the fire temple in Lahore, pure and incandescent on its bed of ashes, formed behind her shut lids. Its glow suffused her with tranquility and strength.(AB, P 317)

Feroza decides not to go back home but live in America. Although the sense of dislocation, of not belonging is more acute in America, she feels it bearable because "it was shared by thousands of newcomers like herself' (AB, P. 312) The attraction of America not only lies in the material comfort but in America 'freedom' is considered a birthright of every individual. If the New World offers Feroza adequate social space to grow, Zoroastrianism provides the ultimate emotional and religious space to her. Nilufer Bharucha has rightly pointed:

> Feroza in *An American Brat* is symbolic of the postcolonial Parsi- especially the post-colonial Parsee-woman who has to battle not just dominant group pressures and their religious fundamentalism, but has also to confront the orthodox patriarchy of her own ethnic group. However the more this ethnic group identity is threatened, the stronger it becomes and in the ultimate analysis it is an identity which is inviolate – as Feroza realized no one could take away her Parsiness from her, not the *mullahs*, not the Parsi orthodoxy, not even enchanting America could destroy it (13)

Though America is full of paradox, she decided to live in America because it provides:

> Privacy, she had come to realize, was one of the prime luxuries the opulence of the first world could provide, as well as the sheer physical space the vast country allowed each individual, each child, almost as a birthright. (AB, P.312)

The technology of the West kept one sufficient unto one's self without the necessity of intrusive human contact. The desire for plenty and privacy has resulted in the loss of human contact and the dwindling family values. The thirst for knowledge that the universities and libraries, filled with books has kindled the curiosity in the mind of Feroza so she is not satisfied with degree in hotel management. She would like to go far: anthropology, psychology, journalism, and astronomy. Feroza was aware of her selfishness but it was a selfishness sanctioned by the values of the prosperous New World in which she wished to dwell. Feroza is aware of shortcoming of America. She criticizes America for its sale of the most lethal weapons to impoverished countries like Pakistan. She also perceives the evil of alcoholism in the adapted land.

America though paradoxical "was shaping a New world, the future in microcosm, the melting pot in which every race and creed was being increasingly represented, compelled to live with and tolerate the "other". (AB-313) Feroza decided to play her role in shaping the future. She would leave always room in her life for generosity and constancy, family attachment. This also marks return to the Zoroastrian faith. Towards the end of the novel, she invokes blessing of Ahura Mazda:

> It wouldn't matter if he was a Parsee or of another faith. She would be surer of herself, and she wouldn't let anyone interfere. It really wouldn't matter; weren't they all children of the same Adam and Eve? As for her religion, no one could take it away from her; she carried its fire in her heart. If the priests in Lahore and Karachi did not let her enter the fire temple, she would go to one in Bombay where there were so many Parsees that no one would know if she was married to Parsi or a none. (AB P.317)

The end of the novel is touchable. She is very optimistic. In her case, the prediction of Fr. Fibs comes true:

> If she flew and fell again, could she pick herself up again? May be one day she'd soar to that self-contained place from which there was no falling, if there was such a place (AB P.317)

V.L.V.N. Narendra Kumar points out that her realization of her creative potential and the resultant shift in her consciousness exemplify the central tenet of Zoroastrianism – the triumph of the forces of good. (14) Feroza's mental turmoil and the quest of identity typify the predicament of the modern multi-cultural society in almost all country. She is also the symbol of youngsters, especially the expatriate ones, striving hard to keep balance between tradition and modernity, past and present, dependent and freedom.

Sidhwa's protagonists are not prisoner of their ethnicities. Feroza and Zareen try to move beyond their ethnicity, try to challenge it and they also interrogate- to hegemonic pressures from the west. Being immigrant they carve their own 'routes' in adopted land. Sidhwa's ethono-religious discourse is thus what Homi Bhabha has called "the social articulation of difference, from the minority perspective". (15) Homi Bhabha writes about ambivalence present in minority discourse:

> Minority discourse sets the act of emergence in the antagonistic in between of image and sign, the accumulative and the adjunct, presence and proxy. It contests genealogies of 'origin' that lead to claims for cultural supremacy and historical priority. Minority discourse acknowledges the status of national culture and the people – as a contentious, performative space of the perplexity of the living in the midst of the pedagogical representations of the fullness of life. Now there is no reason to believe that such marks of difference – the incommensurable time of the subject of culture can not inscribe a 'history' of the people or become the gathering points of political solidarity. They will not however, celebrate the monumentality of historic memory, the sociological solidity or totality of society, or the homogeneity of cultural experience, the discourse of the minority reveals of the insurmountable ambivalence, that structures the *equivocal* movement of historical time (16)

In an increasingly, globalizing world, the concept of diaspora problematises the question of identity. And identity is closely linked to difference. Identity cannot be constructed from a single source; it is complex, contested and always changing. The usual indices of ethnicity are- race, religion, language, nationality and state. Out of these indices the Parsees possess only two identity markers-race and religion. In this age of globalization, information technology and increasing terrorism, ethnicity has become the last refuge. Though western theorists might consider ethnocentrism a form of bias, but western views are wrong when they tend to interpret others peoples, cultures and histories in term of the values of western modernism. The ethnic identity is the identity with which a person is born and it is different from all other multiple identities acquired later in life. Ethnic identity can be rejected but cannot be taken away.

When group's identity clashes with another group–often-dominant group's identity, ethnic clashes are born. These hegemonic forces are not always western or external. In countries like India which is multiethnic, right from the age of king Ashoka and Akbar; where different ethnic group also feel need to assert their ethnicities when confronted with homogenizing dominant groups. Even an extremely westernized community like that of Parsis, has rediscovered its ethnic identity in the face of hegemonic forces. Parsis community is a good example of assimilation with the dominant group because they have done several compromises with the several dominant groups – in pre-colonial, colonial and post-colonial India.

Through the novel *The Crow Eaters,* Sidhwa has depicted Parsi Ethos and assimilation of Parsi community within the Indian subcontinent and in the western countries where they have migrated. The protagonist Faredoon Junglewalla can be regarded as an archetypal migrant. Through Faredoon Jungle Walla, "Freddy for short", Sidhwa highlights how practical and enterprising Parsis are. The migration of Freddie from the central India to Lahore, Karachi, Bombay and London, is not as sweeping and painful as it usually is but it involves certain features of dislocation, displacement and even initial disorientation. Freddie leaves his ancestral village in Central India, in early twentieth century during the British Raj along with his wife Putli, mother-in-law Jerbanoo and his infant daughter Hutoxi. Freddie falls in love with Lahore and gets his family settled in a flat atop his brand-new provision store in one of the most busy and commercially prosperous areas of the city. Gradually, like any migrant, with hard work, resourcefulness and sheer will to succeed, he increases business from his single provision store to a chain of stores, in several North Indian cities and license for "handling all traffic of goods between Peshawar and Afghanistan" (CE P.10)

Of course, Freddie could achieve this success only because of 'fellow-feeling' which is remarkable quality of the Parsi community:

> An endearing feature of this microscopic merchant community was its compelling sense of duty and obligation towards other Parsis. Like on large close-knit family, they assisted each other, sharing successes and rallying to support failure. There were no Parsi beggars in a country abounding in beggars. (CE P.21)

The key of success story of the Freddie lies in his Parsi ethnicity and their policy to make compromises with their dominant ethnic group, which maximizes material and social gains and minimizes survival risk. Like his "august ancestors" who had bowed to the will of Rana 1300 years ago, Freddy "coos" and salaams low **(CE, P.10)** to the British. He is very pragmatic about allying himself with the dominant group in the colonial India:

> And Where, if I may ask, does the sun rise?... No Not in the east. For us it rises and sets in the Englishman's arse. They are our sovereigns! Where do you think we'd be if we did not curry favours? Next to the nawabs, rajas, and prince lings, we are the greatest toadies of the British Empire!...... otherwise, where could we Parsis be? Cleaning out gutters with the untouchables-a dispersed pinch of snuff sneezed from the heterogeneous nostrils of India! Oh Yes, in looking after our interests we have maintained our strength – the strength to advance the grand cosmic plan of Ahura Mazda – the deep spiritual law which governs the universe, the path of *Asha*. *(CE P.12)*

Freddie's migration symbolizes the attempts of Parsees, migrating from the west coast and settling in healthier climate of North Indian cities, in the late nineteenth and the turn of this century. The Novy Kapadia has rightly pointed how *The Crow Eaters* is autobiographical and how history is compelling factor in Sidhwa's creative writing:

> This is the hallmark of Bapsi Sidhwa's work, deceptively perceptive, she accurately depicts historical facts

> interwoven with satirical fiction and lampoon which aptly recreates the Parsee milieu and yet makes for delightful reading. The authenticity of Bapsi Sidhwa's work is evident as she was born in Karachi in 1936, was brought up in Lahore and continues to live there. Her family, the Bhandaras, a leading business family of Lahore for generations, had migrated there in the last century. So Bapsi Sidhwa belongs to the third generation of Parsee settlers in North Indian cities and was reared on talks both fictional and otherwise on the entrepreneurial skill of the elders of her community. Hence her description of the exploits of Faredoon Junglewalla and his family is not just historical fiction, but has a strong autobiographical element also.**(17)**

It is observed that Freddie is not all hesitant of his sycophancy towards British and he is not ashamed of calling himself a "toadies of the British Empire". Freddie's behavior towards Mr. Chareles P. Allen, the deputy commissioner and his frequent visits to the government house to pay homage to the British Empire shows basic attitude of Parsi community to the ruling colonial power. Through the life of Freddie, Sidhwa has carefully shown that Parsees has realized that only their loyalty to ruler will create the political climate in which they could live undisturbed life. The only condition of their loyalty to any ruling groups is that they should not hinder their practice in religion. Freddie shows-how secure Parsees are in self-respect and self-esteem engendered by their identity of a Parsi Zoroastrian, Novy Kapadia has written about this 'sycophancy' which is a 'need to exist' for Parsi:

> Hence the exaggerated servility of Freddy, his son Billy and other Parsees towards British is revealed as an act to ensure security, peace, and economic prosperity. With her ironic perspective the flattery of the Parsees is humorously revealed in the novel, but it also expresses an understanding identity crisis and quest for security amongst the community as a whole. (18)

Though Parsis were equally educated, and extensively anglicized and loyal to the British; Britishers never consider them equal. The Parsi community in India remains the schizophrenic community due to the insecurity and alienation being a minority. Britishers has use Parsi as a broker and reliable trading partner. Parsis try to maintain their own identity, free of both the English and other Indians. Bapsi Sidhwa has witnessed the historical movements in early twentieth century which depict this identity search in several situations in the novel *The Crow Eaters.*

Though Parsis tried to maintain their identity, free from the English and Indians, they couldn't stop the Parsis becoming cultural hybrids in India. They are well-known for their westernization but they have also adopted the customs of Hindus and Muslims both. When Freddie's son Billy and his wife entered in new house, Putli perform the honors on the verandah. Tanya and Billy bowed to her as she swings a silver tray containing water and uncooked rice round their heads. She sacrifices an egg, circling it seven times over their heads. Then she whacks a fresh coconut vigorously until it cracks and spills its water. The same Hindu rituals are also shown when Zareen in *An American Brat* took out three jalapeno peppers from the fridge, and holding them in her fist, draw seven circles in the air over Feroza's head, whispering a hodgepodge of incantations:

> May the mischief of malign and envious eyes leaves you, may the evil in my loving eye leave you, may any magic and ill will across the seven seas be banished, may Ahura Mazda's protection and blessing guard you.(AB, P.303)

Bapsi Sidhwa shows Hindu rituals are blend with the prayers to Ahura Mazda.

Though Parsis were monotheistic, they were fascinated by black magic and Indian astrologers. Freddie consulted an astrologer and this man, correctly foretold the death of his beloved son, Soli. The superstitious belief, evil spirits, astrology are renounced by Zarathushtra. Putli has to go along with Freddie to parties of British people. Sidhwa has depicted how the interaction of two cultures produces tension:

> What revolted Putli most was the demand that she, dutiful and God-fearing wife, must walk a step ahead of her husband. She considered this hypocritical and pretentious, and most barbarous. (CE P.188)

Sidhwa points out the difficulty of Putli to change according the British culture:

> Deep-rooted in the tradition of a wife walking three paces behind her husband, their deportment was as painful to Putli as being marched naked in public (CE P.188)

The gradual assimilation of British culture in Parsis is shown by the change in new generations in the Junglewalla family. New generation with their increasing business contacts with the British has become more westernized. Freddie's youngest son Billy and his fashionable wife Tanya are good example of 'liberal' western culture:

> They entertained continuously at small, intimate 'mixed' parties where married couples laughed and danced decorously with other married couples. 'Mixed' parties were as revolutionary a departure from Freddy's all male get together at the Hira Mandi, and Putli's rigid female sessions, as is discotheque from a Victorian family dinner. The parties were fashionably cosmopolitan, including the various religious sects of India: Hindus, Sikhs, Muslims, Christians, the Europeans, and the Anglo-Indians (CE P.245)

Though highly westernized, Freddie and his son Billy adopt double standards in man and women relationship. Billy wants Tanya to appear westernized and talk English but at home he expects her to be servile and domestic wife. Thus novel highlights Parsi milieu in the throes of change.

The cultural difference is the reality in almost all country. No country can claim of having homogeneous culture. Cultural diversity adds colour and variety to the human world but at the same time it divides people in various groups having little in common with one another. Bapsi Sidhwa has highlighted in all her novels the issue of the cultural difference and problems arising out of it. According to Homi K. Bhabha:

> Cultural difference does not simply represent the contention between oppositional contents or antagonistic traditions of cultural values. Cultural difference introduces into the process of cultural judgment and interpretation that sudden shock of the successive, nonsynchronic time of signification.....Cultural difference marks the establishment of new forms of meaning, and strategies of identification, through process of negotiation where no discursive authority can be established without revealing the difference of itself. The signs of cultural difference can not then be unitary or individual forms of identity because their continual implication in other systems always leaves them 'incomplete' or open to cultural translation.(19)

The cultural difference creates the most humorous situations in Freddie's visit to London along with Putli and his mother-in-law Jerbanoo. The rooms in hotel do not have attached baths. There is one bathroom and three lavatories at the end of their corridor. In the lavatories there are no taps, no water, only flush bowls and toilet paper. The moment Freddy and Putli leave the hotel, Jerbano rushes to lavatory along with her jar. One sunny morning while she is leaning out of her balcony, an idea occurs to her that she can use as bathroom. When she is splashing about happily, she hears a furious voice below: 'Blimey! God, we're being flooded!'*(CE P.268)* Jerbano peers over the balcony into the red, wet and choleric face of an Englishman who demanded: 'Where on earth is all water coming from"*(CE P.268)* Jerbano pointed a prophetic hand at the cloudless sky and thundered: 'Rain! Rain!'*(CE P268)*. A few minutes later the English man knocks her door and demands her to tell what she was doing on the balcony. Jerbano glowered:

> You not poke your nose into me mister, I not poke my nose into you!.........I tell you! I wash my bottom. I no dry-

> clean like you dirty Englishman. I wash my bottom!*(CE P.269)*

The Englishman before leaving the hotel lodges a violent protest with the management.

Freddie, like other Parsis was not in favour of the end of British Empire as he has prospered during the Raj, but the nationalist Parsis such as Dadabhai Naoroji, Phirozshah Mehta and Bhikaji Cama spend their life in apposing British and establishing Indian National Congress. Dadabhai Naoroji cried in presidential address of 1893 to the Indian National Congress:

> Whether I am a Hindu, a Mohomadden, a Parsi, a Christian, or of any other creed, I am above all an Indian Our country is India; our nationality is Indian. (20)

Freddie was unimpressed by Naoroji because he knows after decolonization the Hindus will get their part, Muslims the other, even Sikh, Bengalies, Tamils they may get their part but Parsi will not get any part. The novel *The Crow Eaters* ends with the Parsis quest of identity and their confusion of identity.

The discussion was going between Billy, Ardishir and Bobby Kartak about the repercussion, which Parsis has to face after independence. Bobby Kartak asked: "But what will happen to us? Where will go?" Freddie's answer was "Nowhere my children. We will stay where we are."(CE. 283) Due to the less numerical strength, Parsis cannot expect a homeland separate from Hindus and Muslims territories. So by the end of 1930s they have adopted the principle of neutrality. Freddie ends the discussion softly;

> "We will stay where we are... let Hindus, Muslims, Sikhs or whoever rule. What does it matter? The sun will continue to set-in their arses.....!" (CE-P.283)

The end of British Raj was not simple as Freddie visualizes. The departure of Raj resulted in the partition. Parsis couldn't keep themselves detached from this event. Arundhaty Roy has said in her essay on Globalization that 'You can not remain stable in the moving train', (The Hindu). The novel ends with the note that Parsis policy to be neutral has not helped them.

Sidhwa's novel *The Ice-Candy Man/Cracking India* takes up the narrative from the point that *The Crow Eaters* had left. Talking about the theme of *Cracking India,* Ambareen Hai writes:

> First, self consciously locating itself in Pakistan's border city of Lahore, *Cracking India* explores the traumatic event of partition and the construction of geographical borders (which "cracked" British India into two unforgiving enemies, modern India and Pakistan) to reflect on borders as sites of postcolonial national formation. It questions and ironizes the arbitrary and hurried imposition of borders via a child's anxious naivete (21)

Many novels are written on partition in English but Sidhwa's novel is different. Sidhwa is the first Parsi writer to write on partition, with Parsi perspective and therefore *Cracking India* is more objective than Khushwant Singh's *A Train to Pakistan* and Manohar Malgankar's *A Bend In The Ganges* exhibiting Sikh, Muslim biases respectively. Saros Cowasjee, himself a Parsi writer, writes about the need which Sidhwa has fulfilled by writing *Cracking India*:

> The emotional trauma of the religious minorities such as the Christians, Parsis, and Jews during the partition has not been fully depicted in the Indian English novels. Though unaffected by the communal frenzy, they too were victims of the partition on a religious basis. (22)

The novel depicts the saga of Parsi community against the traumatic backdrop of the division of India. The Parsi identity confusion is that – whether they should show their allegiance to Pakistan or India.

Lenny, a girl child is the narrator of this story. Like Lenny, Bapsi Sidhwa at the time of partition was an eight-year-old girl living in Lahore. This experience was so intense and nightmarying that Sidhwa decided to write a story. Sidhwa tells Feroza Jussawala:

> When I was a child living in Lahore at the time of partition, my maiden name was Bhandara, which sounded like Hindu name. After most of the riots were over, a gang of looters came in carts into our house thinking it's an abandoned house. They were quite shocked to see us and my mother and our Muslim cook came out and said, "What do you damn people think you're doing? This is a Parsi household." And they said, "We thought it was a Hindu household", and they went away. I decide to write a story about partition because this scene was vivid in my mind. (23)

According to Nilufer Bharucha, "Lenny is subaltern figure. She is not just a marginal person, she is marginalized three times over- she is female, belongs to minority community and physically handicapped."*(24)* Sidhwa is a typical postcolonial writer. Through Lenny, She questions the Eurocentric and Andocentric master narratives. Ralp Crane point's out-how Sidhwa subverts "received history" in *The Crow Eaters* and *Ice Candy Man/Cracking India:*

> Sidhwa is also, as a Pakistani writer, writing against Indians views of the past, against predominantly Indian versions of partition, which have increasingly been challenging British interpretation of those events. And as a Parsi, she even appears, on occasions, to write against Pakistani interpretation of history.(25)

Sidhwa's treatment of history is typical of a postcolonial novelist. She was not happy with the literature on the theme of partition written by the British and the Indian writers because they had glorified Gandhi and portrayed Jinnah as a monster. In her interview with Montenegro she tries to defend Jinnah being a Pakistani writer:

> And I felt, in Ice-Candy-Man, I was just redressing in a small way, a very grievous wrong that has been done to Jinnah and Pakistanis by many Indian and British writers. They've dehumanized him, made him a symbol of the sort of person who brought about the partition of India, a person who was hard-headed and obstinate. Whereas,

> in reality, he was the only constitutional man who didn't sway crowds just by rhetoric and tried to do everything by the British standards of constitutional law. (26)

Though Gandhi is glorified throughout the world but Sidhwa has shown him as a tricky politician. Masseur says of Gandhiji, "He's politician. It's his business to suit his tongue to moment." (CI P.91) Colonel Bharucha who had earlier denounced the British for bringing strange western diseases to India (Lenny's 'polio') also turns with anger to the Indian Nationalist: "Gandhi says we must stop buying salt. We should only eat salt manufactured from the Indians Ocean!... Who does Gandhi think he is?"*(CI P.35)* Kashmir has always been a bone of contention between India and Pakistan. According Sidhwa the British have shown favour to Nehru by granting him Kashmir. Sidhwa depicts Nehru thus:

> Nehru wears red carnations in the buttonholes of his ivory jackets. He bandies words with Lady Mountbatten and is presumed to be her lover. He is charming, too, to Lord Mountbatten. Suave, Cambridge polished, he carries about him an aura of power and a presence that flatters anyone he complements tenfold. He doles out promises, smiles kisses-on-cheeks. He is the prime of his Brahmin manhood. He is handsome, his cheeks glow pink (CI P.159)

Before partition people of all communities live happily. Lenny use to observe:

> One day everybody is themselves and the next day they are Hindu, Muslim, Sikh, Christian. People shrink, dwindling into symbols. (CI P.93)

The fever of partition catch cities first and than it came to villages, Lenny as a child could not believe that the same people who were ready to give their life for each other have become their own enemies. Though Parsis were not the victims of partition their agony was as intense as Hindus, Muslims and Sikhs. In *The Crow Eaters* Freddie has advised Parsis to be neutral. But Dr. Modi questions the neutrality of Parsis... "How can we remain uninvolved, our neighbours will think we are betraying them and siding with the English?"

One of the practical souls asks with an impatient voice, "Which of your neighbours are you going to betray? Hindu? Muslim? Sikh?"(CI P.37) Thus Sidhwa highlights the identity crisis of the Parsi community on the eve of partition. Lenny couldn't believe "India is going to be broken. Can one break country?" (CI P.92)

Sidhwa re-examines the role of the British in cracking the country in to Pakistan and India. The Birth of Pakistan leads to an identity crisis in Lennie. She observes, "I am Pakistani. In a snap, Just like that."(CI P.140) The discussion between Col. Bharucha, Dr. Mody reminds in the novel the history of the Parsi Diasporic community which has left Iran to settle in India. The core of the discussion was on the eve of partition - where they should go? Should they go to other countries? But Col. Bharucha thundered, "Do you think it is easy to be accepted in a new country? It was ultimately decided:

> As long as we do not interfere we have nothing to fear! As long as we respect the customs of our rulers as we always have- we'll be all right! Ahura Mazda has looked after us for thirteen hundred years. He will look after us for another thirteen hundred! (CT P.39)

Even after this discussion some were hesitant to live in a Muslim country. Some of them have given a solution to migrate to Bombay or London. Dr. Mody shouted:

> And what do we do when the English king's Vazir stands before us with a glassful of milk? Tell him we are brown Englishmen, come to sweeten their" lives with a dash of colour? (CI P.40)

Colonal Bharucha ends the discussion:

> "As long as we conduct our lives quietly, as long as we present no threat to anybody, we will prosper right here. (CI P.40)

The above discussion about their migration, instability of their living highlights the pangs of Parsi community and their question of existence after partition.

Lenny is the representative of the Parsi community. With the creation of the Muslim state of Pakistan, her world became limited; it lost its Hindus and Sikhs. In *An American Brat*, Feroza was sent to America because for Parsis, their biggest fear was that their girls would marry Muslim boys. According to Keki N. Daruwalla:

> Bapsi Sidhwa is more down to earth. Lahore was a mosaic of many communities (27)

Sidhwa is a comprehensive writer who writes almost of all communities Sikhs, Muslims, Hindus, Christians, and Jews.

Thus in *Cracking India* Sidhwa rejects the British and pro-Hindu versions of history. Discussing the treatment of history in postcolonial fiction, Ashcroft, Griffiths and Tiffin content that, "received history is tampered with. It is rewritten and realigned from the victims of its destructive progress" (28) Thus, Sidhwa rewrites the history in the *Cracking India*. In another words, it can be said in Rushdie's expression she, "writes back to the centre"

Ambareen Hai has rightly pointed:

> Recent feminist and postcolonial work in particular has turned to the crossing and inhabiting of borders by third world women writers in an effort to reconsiders their strategies of survival as they negotiate-often subversively-the contradictions of cultural heterogeneity, modernity, nationalism or diasporic identity. (29)

Ambareen Hai has also marked that in a recent postcolonial work a focus is not only on boundary crossing but also on border inhabitation. Homi Bhabha describes the border space as the productive 'tenebrousness' of the 'interstitial', or the 'in-between':

> These in-between spaces provide the terrain for elaborating strategies of selfhood-singular or communal-that initiate new signs of identity and innovative sites of collaboration, and contestation, in the act of defining the idea of society itself. (30)

He continues,

> It is the space of intervention emerging in the cultural interstices that introduces creative invention into existence (31)

Like her character in the fiction, Sidhwa herself occupies several positions. She has always lived in Pakistan, though she now lives in US. She belongs to the minority Parsee or Zoroastrian community to which Homi Bhabha, the major proponent of hybridity belongs. This historically diasporic community (exiled from Persia since the seventh century), which is ethnically distinct, has made Sidhwa a post-colonial writer. Her novel *Cracking India* is a postcolonial text, which can be seen both as a border crosser and border inhabitant.

Sidhwa's first novel (though the second to be published), *The Bride*, portrays the multiple displacements forced by the partition. Partition with the inevitable, "dis-location" acts as a recurrent motif in *The Bride*. Over a million people died during this "dislocational" event. Sidhwa reveals the incredible misery caused by this event. The repercussions of the partition were not only on the national level but also on the personal level, which has made people 'liminal' figure even today. The personal life of the comman people was transformed, wrecked. Sidhwa shows through the novel that the partition is continuous, unexpected and often forced dislocation not only from a familiar place but also from cultures and people.

Quasim is the first character in the book that is exposed to the ravages of "partition". He is forced, through circumstances, which are totally beyond his control, to "dislocate" to a totally alien landscape, people and culture. Quasim goes to Jullunder, gets a job as watchman at bank and lives there for three years. In the wake of partition violence, he kills Giridharilar (who has insulted him) and boards a train to Pakistan. Zaitoon, a Punjabi child, the main heroine of the novel is introduced, along with her Muslim parents, Sikander and Zohra, who are forced to flee to Pakistan. Her parents are killed among others in front of her eyes by the Sikhs. Zaitoon blindly runs to Quasim and calls him 'Abba'.

As *The Crow Eaters* was set in the marginalized Parsi community, *The Bride* was set in another marginalized ethnic group of Pakistan. Quasim's marginalized position as a Kohistani tribal is made clear at the outset of the novel. When Zaitoon is fifteen, she is taken to Kohistan to be married to one of his kinsmen (Sakhi) by Quasim. She is 'used' as sacrifice to re-establish his link with his homeland and then she is left in a totally alien and hostile environment. Sakhi, in accordance with the expectations of a man's role in Kohistani traditions, starts the frequent and brutal beating in order to "tame" Zaitoon when she dares to go against his wishes. Before Sakhi kills her, Zaitoon has decided to run away from Kohistan. As she runs away from the village, the tribe considers it as their 'dishonour' and decided to kill her. With barely enough food and blanket, she ventures through the unfamiliar hills towards the bridge across the river. Vultures begin to trail her. She hasn't eaten anything for days. Finally bruised, raped, half-dead, after ten days, she is spotted by the army and carrying her bundled up in her old blanket. The Major makes his way across his own territory. Sakhi follows him but went back when Mushtaq tells him that girl is dead. Regarding the future of Zaitoon, Major Mushtaq has two possibilities in his mind:

> She would be all right, he mused. In a few hours he would quietly stow her away in the vehicle taking Farrukh and Carol to Lahore. Let Carol take care of her! She could hide in the States! Or perhaps Ashiq could propose marriage after a decent interval- she would be as securely hidden in his village. (TB P.245)

As Sidhwa shows multiple displacements of Zaitoon, she also shows American character-Carol dislocated from her home and culture in America. She is totally alien in Pakistan. Carol is a typically middle-class American of the sixties by birth and upbringing. While working as a sales girl in a cosmetic store, she meets Farrukh, a Pakistani engineering student, and falls in love with him. Carol is not able to cope up with the repressed sexuality of Pakistani society where she is constantly pressurized by men. Her westernized habits of social intercourse are misinterpreted by her husband and the men she meets. Carol tried to adjust with some aspects of

Pakistani culture. Farrukh Khan has rightly pointed the reason of Carol's stay in Pakistani. He writes:

> Carol chooses to stay in Pakistan because she is able to have an identity, which would have been non-existent if she had continued to work as a shop assistant in a department store in San Jose. Sidhwa conveys the fear and boredom of a single woman worker by making Carol stay in Pakistan, with its alien and sometimes claustrophobic culture, rather than return to the drudgery of American life that she would lead if she chose to go back. (32)

But the end of the novel shows-Carol's journey back to her home. Carol was shocked when Major Mushtaq casually says about the condition of Zaitoon:

> It happens all the time... Oh! Women get killed for one reason or other... imagined insults, family honour, infidelity...(TB P.223)

As Carol loves Mushtaq, she is horrified. She asked Mushtaq,

> Do you think Farrukh would kill me? He answers, "Who knows? I might, if you were my wife. (TB P.224)

Carol realizes, like Zaitoon, she is also exploited. She thinks about women's condition in the world, especially in Pakistan. She asks Farukh to explain the word 'Khudi' used by Iqbal in famous verse. Farukh explains,

> Khudi- It's your will power. No, more than just will power or ego. It's the strength of nature-a force, perhaps of God, within one. (TB P.228-229)

Carol remembers-how Zaitoon has exercised her "Khudi". She says to Farukh:

> I think I'm finally beginning to realize something...Your civilization is too ancient...too different... and it has ways that can hurt me... really hurt me... I'm going home. 'Lahore?' San Jose. (TB, P.229)

It is love for life that compels Carol, to dissolve her marriage and go back to America. Zaitoon, inspite of the brutality decided to live life. The prime concern of Sidhwa's women is the preservation of life. According Ralph J. Crane:

> Her (Carol) presence in the novel does not emphasize the cross-cultural differences between East and West so much as the cross-gender difference that exist within Pakistani society.(33)

Sidhwa's protagonists are mostly women, who question the narrow and constricting roles assigned to them in the name of 'honours', 'shame' and 'modesty'. Sidhwa, in the novel, *The Bride* provides an alternative voice which subverts the roles assigned to women of Pakistan. Kumkum Sangari and Sudesh Vaid have explained the concept of a "feminist historiography" in introduction to *Recasting Women*:

> Historiography may be feminist without being, exclusively, women's history such a historiography acknowledges that each aspect of reality is gendered, and thus involved in questioning all that we think we know, in a sustained examination of analytical and epistemological apparatus, and in dismantling of the ideological presupposition of so called gender neutral methodologies. A feminist historiography rethinks historiography as a whole and discards the idea of women as something to be framed by a context in order to be able to think of gender difference as both structuring and structured by the wide set of social relations (34)

Bapsi Sidhwa rigorously questions the histories and the assumptions of contemporary Pakistani/Indian society, American society through her fiction. She gives voice to various marginalized groups of India and Pakistan.

REFERENCES

1. Daruwala Keki N., "Of Parsis and Their Literature", Critical Practice: *A Journal of Critical and Literary Studies*, Vol. VII Jan 2000. Ed. Avadeshkumar Singh. Delhi, p. 92.
2. Cicely Havely, "Patterns of Migration", *The Novels of Bapsi Sidhwa* Ed. R. K. Dhawan and Novy Kapadia. Prestige 1996, p. 69.

3. *Ibid.,* p. 69.
4. *Ibid.,* p. 62.
5. Bharucha Nilofer E, "Resisting Colonial and Post-colonial Hegemonies: Bapsi Sidhwa's Ethno-Religious Discourse", *Asian American Writing* Vol. No. II ed. Somnath Mandal, Prestige Books New Delhi 2000, p. 94.
6. Hussain Naila, "On the Writer's World", Interview with Bapsi Sidhwa, *The Nation, Midweek*, 26 May 1993, p. 19.
7. Ashcraft, Griffiths and Tiffin, *The Empire Writes Back* London Rutledge 1989, p. 8-9.
8. Kirpal Vinay, *The Third World of Expatriation.* New Delhi Sterling 1989, p. 5.
9. Narendrakumar V.L.V.N., "Westernization and Expatriation", *Parsee Novel* Pretige Books. New Delhi 2002, p. 14.
10. Kirpal Vinay *op. cit.,* p. 88.
11. Villareal Edit, "Feroza Goes Native." *The Washington Post,* Dec.16.1993, p. 89.
12. Bharucha Nilufer *op. cit.,* p. 98.
13. Bharucha Nilufer *op. cit.,* p. 100.
14. Narendrakumar V.L.V.N. *op. cit.,* p. 68.
15. Bhabha Homi K., "*The Location of Culture*". London: Routledge, 1994, p. 2.
16. Bhabha Homi K., " Dissemination: Time, Narrative and the Margins of the Modern Nation", *Nation and Narration.* London: Routledge, 1990, p. 307-308.
17. Kapadia Novy, "The Parsee Pradox in Bapsy Sidhwa's",*The Crow Eaters, The Novels of Bapsi Sidhawa*, ed. R. K. Dhawan. and Novy. Kapadia. Prestige 1996, p. 126.
18. *Ibid.,* p. 127.
19. Bhabha Homi K. *op. cit., Nation and Narration* 1994, p. 313.
20. Villarreal Edit. *op. cit.*, p. 90.
21. Hai Ambareen, "Border Work, Border Trouble: Postcolonial Feminism And The Ayah in Bapsi Sidhwa's Cracking India", *Modern Fiction studies.* Sum.2000. Pub. by John. Hopkins University Press, p. 388.
22. Cowsjee Saros, "The Partition in Indo-English", *Exploration in Modern Indo-English Fiction*, ed. R.K. Dhawan.(New Delhi : Bahri 1982) p. 29.
23. Feroza Jussawalla and Reed Way Dasenbroole. ed. Interviews with Writers of the Post-colonial World. *Jackson and London: University Press of Mississippi.* 1992 : p. 200.

24. Bharucha E. Nilufer, "From Behind A Fine Veil. A Feminist Reading of Three Parsi Novels", *Indian Literature Sahitya Akadami's* Bi-Monthly. Journal, p. 132.
25. Crane Ralph J., "A Passion of History and for Truth Telling : The Early Novels of Bapsi Sidhwa". *The Novels of Bapsi Sidhawa*, ed R.K. Dhawan and Novy Kapadia, ed R.K. Dhawan and Novy Kapadia, New Delhi. Prestige Books, 1996, p. 50.
26. Montenegro David, "Bapsi Sidhwa: An Interview". The *Massachusetts. Review* Winter (1990) p. 532.
27. Daruwala Keki. N., "Looking Back Coming to Terms with History". Review on Partition Dialogues: Memories of a lost Home. Alok Bhalla. Literary Review. *The Hindu* Sunday May 7,2006.
28. Ashcraft, Griffiths and Tiffin. *op. cit.*, p. 57.
29. Hai Ambareen. *op. cit.*, p. 381-82
30. Bhabha Homi K. *op. cit.*, (The Location of Culture.) p. 1-2.
31. Bhabha Homi K. *op. cit.*, (The Location of Culture) p. 9.
32. Khan Farrukh, "Women, Identity and Dislocation in The Bride", *The Novels of Bapsi Sidhwa* ed. R.K. Dhawan and Novy Kapadia Prestige. pp. 144-145.
33. Crane Ralph J. *op. cit.*, p. 51.
34. Sangari Kumkum and Vaid Sudesh, "Recasting Women: An Introduction", *Recasting Women: Essays in Colonial History*. ed. Kumkum Sangari and Sudesh Vaid. New Jersey: Rutgers University, Press 1989, p. 3.

Chapter 3

Nationalism, Transnationalism, Liminality

Diasporic Experience in Chitra Banerjee Divakaruni

The South Asian Diaspora constitutes a minority discourse, surfacing with urgency in the field of cultural studies in the US. Though it is the fourth-largest Asian American community, the historians, social scientists and politicians neglect it. This forced invisibility and negligence is challenged by the contemporary South Asian writers like Chitra Banerjee, Meena Alexander, Jhumpa Lahiri. The invisibility, racism and loss of identity are very poignant experience for the immigrant. The 'immigrant right movement' has started in the US. Recently on May 1, hundreds of thousands of immigrants all over the US kept away from the work, school and shopping to demonstrate their economic power. The powerful business as well as labor interest has supported this movement because large sectors of the American economy would grind to an abrupt halt without the cheap labor of these immigrants. It is the paradox that on one hand America prides itself being a nation of immigrants and on the other hand immigration has become a difficult issue for the US. From the recent address of President Bush on television it seems that immigration has become the political issue hotter even than the Iraq war.

Contemporary diasporic writers do not carry their India with them wherever they go and they never blend in to the American melting pot like Bharti Mukherjee. Debjani Banerjee has rightly pointed out the way contemporary South Asian writers make their space in US:

> Contemporary writing from the south Asian diaspora bears the marks of a cultural encounter that combines the rewriting of history with nuanced responses to dislocation and marginalization by hegemonic structures. The raw energy of first generation politics is substituted by a more complex response to issues of race and unbelonging. The new writers retort to their attempted marginalization, not by dissolving into mainstream but by rendering their distinctive voices. [1]

The women writers of Indian diaspora are the product of two cultures, they are unsure of their status related tc mainstream and also in relation to their minority group. Manju Jaidka writes about the empowerment of these women writers:

> Grappling with the problem of defining their identities, the self they depict is a confused one, some times central and sometimes the marginalized other, although their effort is to move from margin to center. Such a move may lead to an empowerment of themselves. [2]

Though, these women writers of Indian diaspora live on the peripheries of the mainstream culture they provide empowered space that promises to create new subjectivities, new identities in US. Homi Bhabha writes about this 'in-between' space in his essay, "Dissemination: time, narrative and the margins of the modern nation":

> The boundary that secures the cohesive limits of the western nation may imperceptibly turn into a contentious internal liminality that proves a place from which to speak both of, and, as, the minority, the exilic, the marginal and the emergent. [3]

It is this location or 'in-between' space which has turned in an advantages and which has given leading women writers of Indian origin in America such as Bharti Mukherjee, Kiran Narayan, Chitra Divakaruni, Bharti Kirchner and Meena Alexander. These women writers try to present two different worlds simultaneously as they cannot forget past. There is nostalgia for a world left behind combined with the necessity of forging a new identity. Chitra Banerjee deliberately evokes the world left behind and contrasts it with the new, adopted country. Divakaruni reconstruct personal and national histories as historical intervention into master narratives imposed upon her by dominant culture. Histories and memories are not sufficient for survival in the new land one must remake oneself. To write their stories, the pangs of dislocation, the angst experienced during the process of becoming a foreign citizen – the diasporic writer use autobiographical mode for expression. Chitra Banerjee has use the fictional autobiography where the first person narration provides an impression of autobiographical narration even when this is not the case. This new genre is widely handled by immigrant women writers who strive to break away from racial and patriarchal confinements.

In 1991, with a group of friends, Divakaruni founded a help line to provide services to Indian American women. The most important thing the help line volunteers do is to listen and be an empathetic presence. Inspired by the life stories of these women, Divakaruni published a short story collection, *Arranged Marriage* (1995), which told of their abuse and courage. *Arranged Marriage* is Divakaruni's debut in short fiction but it reads as if she has been writing stories all her life. It was as an educator that Divakaruni first began emphasizing communications between cultures. She says:

> I have been teaching for about ten years now. It's a big part of my life, and I have liked teaching from multi-cultural perspective even before it became a big thing [4]

As a pioneer in the field she had to create her own textbooks, including the anthology *Multitude* which she uses for her freshman classes. Scott Lanfort, who teaches English composition and Gay-Lesbian Literature at Foothill College, started with the first edition of *Multitude* and is upgrading to the second edition, comments on it:

> What I think is unique about this book is that the writer speaks to all sides of the human condition.... Not only

> oppression but success and survival. It's about finding a place in a complex world. [5]

The woman as immigrant dominates Divakaruni's first collection of short stories, *Arranged Marriage*. Except for the opening India based selection that sets the mood and establishes the recurring theme, each story takes place in various parts of the United States. They all explore the subtle psychological dominance and the plain physical brutality frequently directed towards South Asian women, whose subjugation is sanctioned by India's patriarchal system. Divakaruni chooses to examine the world of middle class women, housewives, and professionals in *Arranged Marriage.* The stories are about women in relationship, struggling to avoid an arranged marriage, coping within a western marriage, considering prospect of doing without marriage altogether. In these stories even the women who love their husband and lovers find themselves undone by them. Few of these characters find themselves defeated. They prepare to battle the conventions they have left behind to take full advantage of their lives in America.

In the story "Clothes" from *Arranged Marriage,* the husband of narrator, Sumita dies and she is faced with the decision of staying in America or going back to India to live with in-laws. Sumita contemplates:

> That's when I know I can't go back. I don't know yet how I shall manage, here in this new, dangerous land. I only know I must. Because all over India, at this very moment widows in white saries are bowing their veiled heads, serving tea to in-laws. Doves with cut-off wings. [AM 33]

Thus Chitra Banerjee shows how young bride whose fairy tale vision of California is shattered when her husband is murdered in racial attack at his shop and how she decided to run her husband's shop. Sumita's decision of staying in America rather than going back to India along with her in-laws as their daughter, rest of her life shows how she had carved her own 'route' in an alien land. Her husband Somesh wanted to westernize her and he used to bring dresses of American style and always tells her: " I want you to go college, choose a career" [AM-31]

By presenting Sumita, growing with the passage of time during this tragedy in America; retaining her culture in dress and values, as well as assimilating the American culture for personal growth and fulfilling her husband's dream and ultimately deciding to stay in America which made her confident...... Divakaruni shows that all migrants carve their own 'routes' in the course of time and it is not necessary they want to settle in the countries of their origin. Thus new subjectivities are born, the migrants go 'beyond' the binary fixities of natives/migrants and carve new 'route' instead of lamenting over the lost roots as Homi Bhabha theorizes in his *The Location of Culture.*

The majority of the stories in the collection are concerned with changed perspectives on women identities. Though this change is painful it is inevitable. Foroza Jussawalla describes the plight of women immigrants:

> We are like 'chiffon saris' a sort of cross-breed attempt to adjust to the pressure of a new world, while actually being from an older one [6]

In "Affair" Abha the perfect wife and homemaker, realizes that the concept of duty gradually loses its stranglehold in the new country. She leaves security of her loveless marriage and the beauty and calmness of her kitchen for vagaries of a life of struggle. When she ventures on her own, she decides to use her culinary skills to earn financial independence. Before leaving her home she went to her friend Meena who has an affair with some one and is on the way of getting divorced. Abha was doubtful whether Meena has an affair with her husband Ashok but Meena made it clear by showing the photograph of Charles, an ordinary, middle aged man with kind eyes and a bald spot, no better-looking than her husband Shrikant. Meena gives the reason why she wants to get married with Charles:

> But he understands me, even the bad parts, with him I can be myself, like I never could before this. [AM. 269]

To enjoy the 'freedom' and 'individual space' in US Meena is ready to break her arranged marriage which one Indian may find strange. After listening Meena, Abha asked herself:

> Had I ever really been myself? I didn't think so. All my energy had been taken up in being a good daughter, a good friend, and of course a good wife. [AM 269]

Abha contends with her parent's anger, family dishonour, gossip and yet she must leave because. "The old rules aren't always right. Not here, not even in India' [AM 270] . In the fiction of Chitra Banerjee, connections between women consolidate the flatform from which women struggle to find their identity. In 'Affair' the relationship between Abha and Meena builds up the space of interventions that enable both women to extricate themselves from meaningless relationships and rewrite their strategies of survivals.

In "Meeting Mrinal" the protagonist Asha is always in touch with her childhood, career-oriented friend Mrinal (who is unmarried) by sending her letters, photograph of her happy married life. Mrinal works in one computer firm in Bombay. She came to attend a technology transfer conference in San Francisco. After twenty years they met and both found each other very lucky. Asha never told the truth that her husband Mahesh had left her to marry Jessica. Even her teenage son Dinesh avoided her. When Mrinal called her to tell the news of her arrival at San Francisco, next week, Asha told that she is busy with her husband though he never lives with her. Dinesh, her son became irritated and burst out: "Why couldn't you just tell her the fucking truth that he got tired of you and left you for another woman" [AM 283]

Asha manufactures stories that reflect an ordered perfection that her life, in reality, lacks. At the end of the story she realizes this perfection she desired is co-related with her efforts at adhering to traditional values, which her mother taught:

> I think of how hard I always tried to be the perfect wife and mother, like the heroines of mythology I grew up on-patient, faithful Sita, selfess Kunti. [M. 298]

The story "Meeting Mrinal", shows how Divakaruni's characters grapple with and refute an essential identity linked to cultural roots. Asha is unable to live up to the stress of being the perfect wife and mother. Though she tried hard to be a perfect wife, Mahesh left her to get "real happiness" with Jessica.

In *Nation and Narration,* Homi Bhabha writes about the moment when discourses of nationhood re-write themselves in the diaspora:

> History may be half-made because it is in the process of being made and the image of cultural authority may be ambivalent because it is caught, 'uncertainty' in the act of 'composing' its powerful image... The marginal or minority is not the space of a celebratory or utopian, self marginalization. It is a much more substantial intervention into those justifications of modernity – progress, homogeneity, cultural organicism, the deep nation, the long past that rationalize the authoritarian, 'normalizing' tendencies within cultures, in the name of the national interest or ethnic perogative. In this sense, then the ambivalent, antagonistic perspective of nation as narration will establish the cultural boundaries of the nation so that they may be acknowledged as 'containing' thresholds of meaning that must be crossed, erased, and translated in the process of cultural production. [7]

The convenient descriptions of tradition are significant in the diaspora while defining a community in flux. Debjani Banerjee comments on the stories in *Arranged Marriage:*

> In the stories of the *Arranged Marriage* the challenge to normative narratives of nationhood is launched through the explorations of female subjectivity. The diasporic community valorizes an unquestioned perpetuation of traditions through even the most banal signifiers in the name of combating the colonizing influence of the

dominant culture on the one hand, and the contaminating influence of other minority groups on the other. When confronted with the threat of co-optation and assimilation (real or perceived) by discourses regarded as "western" or other, South Asian communities use women as a historic signifying objects who are made to be the bearers of culture. Women, on whose bodies cultures are mapped and re-mapped become the targets of protection – read enhanced patriarchal controls so that they continue to function as stable signifiers of womanhood for a community anxious about preserving its identity in foreign soil. [8]

Circumscribed by such markers of traditional identity, women find themselves living their lives as symbols of national/communal identity, symbols that are easily challenged in the home country but acquire a particular charge in the diaspora. They create their own space where they can articulate their desire. Divakaruni's protragonist's space is necessarily located outside of competing paradigms of traditional identity and modern identity. "Silver pavements and Golden Roofs" one of the earlier stories in collection, reads the diasporic experience in terms of race, there by exploding many myths that texture immigrant life Jayanti's romantic expectation about her life in America evolve around reading American literature and being courted by American professors. She can't comprehend uncle's suppressed anger about America until she became the victim of the violent raciest assault in the street of Chicago. A similar attack had destroyed her uncle's business and put them under a financial strain. Her uncle once tries to tell her the reason of his suppressed anger for America:

> The Americans hate us. They are always putting us down because we are dark - skinned foreigners, *kala admi* Blaming us for the damn economy, for taking away their jobs. You will see it for yourself soon enough [AM-43]

Meena Alexander writes in *The Shock of Arrival:* "The streets lined with gold are hard to walk" [9]. Jayanti finds out "a prince from a far-off magic land, where the pavements are silver and the roofs all gold" (AM 46), shouts, insults, hurts, and slush. Her experience of powerlessness provides her with the prism with which she can view race and class relations and understands what it means to be South Asian in North America.

Divakurani's story "*A Perfect Life* brings out contradictions in America. Meera an immigrant from India shows- how assimilation is difficult for women in U. S. Meena in the beginning feels she lives the 'perfect life'- enjoying an interesting professionals job at the bank, "a tall and lean and sophisticated" (AM-73) white boy friend (of her dream, she has in India) named Richard, designers clothes, fitness routines, a well appointed apartment, and above all her own reckoning freedom. She says:

> What I like most about Richard was that he gave me space.......Richard continued to be passionate without getting possessive. He didn't mind if I went out with my other friends... Thanks to the pill and easy going attitude (it was a Californian thing, he told me once), for the fist time in my life I felt free". (AM-74)

Meena's mother used to send every month the photograph of young handsome Indian boy. For years she had been trying for arranged marriage of her daughter but Meena rejects all parental attempts at arranged marriage, gets on the Pil and try to become completely American. She notes with pride:

> "When I was with Richard I felt like a true American" (AM-73); with him she at least in part plays the vote of exotic oriental wearing a "blue silk kimono".... And I would thank God for my life, which was a civilized as much in control, as *perfect*, as a life could ever be". (AM-77)

At this point Meena is completely identified with her fictional sister Jyoti/Jasmine/Jaze/Jane in Bharti Mukherjee's *Jasmine*. She is in her own mind, the exceptional Asian American women who deserves all that she enjoys because she takes advantage of all the opportunities offered by her new country.

All is well, until a mysterious boy, literally materializes on her doorsteps. Though she declares, in the beginning of the story that she is completely American; she couldn't ignore the boy, at her door step, she ends up taking him in and teaching him how to live in "civilized" society. Her "motherhood" which she has suppressed (unwillingly) to become a "complete" American is evoked and she gave way to her motherhood. She begins procedures to adopt him legally. She names him Krishna which can be shortened to Kris, phonetically indistinguishable from Chris (Suitable in US). The Statue of Liberty in America symbolizes – promising "world-wide welcome" But this generosity is belied by acts of legislative rejection. Their rejection shows that good intentions to take care of the boy are not enough. The birth certificates, medical records, travel papers and other proofs of identity are required for adoption. What is strange in all this process, conflict of adoption is that Meera's boyfriend Richard stays away as a matter of personal feelings and life-style choice.

Regarding Kris's muteness throughout this story, Sau-ling C. Wong writes:

> Kris's muteness throughout; and his "unreadable" (AM97) face the night before he is to be abandoned in the foster care system, suggest that in the American context there is ultimately no discourse available to the "Wretched refuse" of the world to articulate their trauma. Their history is unspeakable and, to borrow Judith Butler's term, culturally unintelligible. [10]

In the end suppressing her grief, she settles for becoming more white moving up to a "bigger, better apartment….with white carpeting and bleached scandinavian furniture to match", and planning to marry Richard on condition that they will not have any children.(AM-107) The end of the story shows that sometime her "motherhood" evokes though she never tells about this to any one. She says:

> And when I come back to my apartment, I close my eyes before the last bend of the stairs that lead to my door. I

> hold my breath and imagine a boy in a red Mickey Mouse T-shirt sitting on the topmost step. *If I can count to twenty, thirty, forty without letting go, I say to myself, he will be there. He will hold out his arms, and in his high, clear voice he will call to me.* I stand there halfway up the darkening staircase feeling the emptiness swirl around, me, my lungs burning, my eyes shut tight as though in prayer. (AM -108)

This seems to suggest that the Asian American woman can secure her place in American society only by loosing (even if unwillingly) her ties to 'huddled masses', or even, that such ties are structurally impossible. There is no 'proper channel' for assimilation of Kris in American body politic.

In the story "Doors" the narrator Preeti falls in love with Deepak who came to US for University education. Her mother apposed their marriage because Preeti was brought up in America. Her mother urged: "its never too late to stop your self from ruining your life, what do you *really* know about how Indian men think? About what they expect from their women?" (AM-184)

Deepak's Indian friends also warned him when they received a wedding invitation:

> *Yaar* are you sure you are doing the right thing? ... She's been here so long it's almost like she was born in this country. And you know how there 'American' women are? Always bossing you, always thing about themselves. It's no wonder we call them ABCDs... American-Born confused –Desis [AM-188]

Though it was the marriage of choice, it disintegrates because being brought up in US, Preeti has developed a Western love of privacy. The couple was perfectly matched until the arrival of Deepak's cousin Raju, in US. He shared their condominium for 18 months while he attends graduate schools. The lack of space suffocates Preeti. She couldn't concentrate on her Ph. D. work. Often she feels asleep over books and woke up to the sound of Deepak's irritated knocks on the doors. Deepak could not understand the reason of Preeti's locking the door of bedroom:

> "I just don't understand you now days!" ...why must you lock the bedroom door when you are reading? Isn't that being a bit paranoid? May be you should see someone about it" [AM-198]

In presence of his cousin, Raju, Deepak's traditional self emerges strongly and the myth of "the enlighten man" (AM-194) crumbles. Preeti in her mind says "Mother, you were right". (AM-200) The conjugal clash between Deepak and Preeti is a confrontation between two cultures, which cannot be resolved.

The stories in *Arranged Marriage* bring out multivalent tensions, which diasporic identities have to face, where value and norms are always in flux. In the story "The Word Love", the intense bond between mother and child is scattered when narrator starts living with her American boyfriend, Rex. The Narrator is torn-up between the traditional Indian ethos and Western understandings of the word, 'love'. Thus Divakaruni's character in *Arranged Marriage* constantly struggle with dual identities and values. Living in sin, indulging in a extramarital affair, the issue of personal space and the real meaning of love.....these are some concerns, author discussed in the stories. These concerns have a completely different shade of meaning in a Indian context. She presents the interpretation of these issues in a Western context. Her characters examine these concerns in the light of their evolving identities as American citizens and make choices that reveal a new emerging reality. Sethi R. C. comments on the relevance short story collection *Arranged Marriage:*

> Her experience with poetry (three books worth) endows these stories with imagery and emotion that linger long after the book has been read. Divakaruni joins Bharti Mukherjee, Anjana Appachana and others as a chronicler of this new wave of immigration. In so doing she creates a book highly appropriate for courses on women's studies as well as multiculturalism. These stories will enrich any course in contemporary literature or the short story, and will, most importantly, continue to open up the world of Indian women to the American reader. (11).

The theme of desire is a continuing one in all her books. The Eastern philosophy moved around the theme of desire. We all have different desires. Some time desire changes us and some time we change desires. According Divakaruni there is lot of difference in Eastern society and Western society. Eastern society is so family oriented that you completely give up your individual desires for the good of the family. In the western society people are individualistic. They never do any compromise with their desires. If the family doesn't agree with them they forget the family.

In the short story collection *The Unknown Errors of our Lives* (2001) the theme of desire is at crux. The characters in these short stories are exposed to both Eastern and Western thinking. They are constantly trying to figure out these thinking in their mind. Divakaruni used a short story form to bring out to life, a complex array of south Asian characters and their struggles to survive within the restrictive social conditions of a rural and urban India and a suburban USA. In this collection some tales are set in India and some are in America. Most of the stories illuminate the pain, loss, and alienation of the immigrant experience.

"Mrs. Dutta writes a Letter" has been selected for Best American short stories, 1919, where a widow living in her son's California home discovers that her old world ways are an embarrassment to her daughter in-law. Divakaruni explores the feeling at the elderly parents who leave their homes and life style in India, to come and stay with their children. Mrs. Dutta didn't like to store the unwashed clothes. In the absence of her daughter-in-law, she washes clothes and hangs on the fences; which was objectionable to an American neighbors. This made her daughter-in-law angry who all these years was taking care "not to give Americans chance to say some thing like this and now…." (UE-29) Mrs. Datta who overhears these words is deeply afflicted but she never demonstrates her embarrassment and lives the normal life. She realizes the reality that "how alone she is in this land of young people and how unnecessary". (UE-33)

Leela, the protagonist of the story "The Lives of Strangers" is brought up in US. Her parents themselves solitary individuals, had encouraged her taste for privacy. The same privacy resulted in her brief affair with Dexter. Even Dexter also wonders that she doesn't need him; in fact she doesn't need *anyone*. But after the suicide attempt, her encounter with death, she for the first time found her own company inadequate. However she decides to go to India. She knows India only through her imagination as a vast and vague, talismanic country. Though her parent's stories had spanned many topics – from the lives of famous scientists to the legend of Greece and Rome, they never discussed their homeland. She lands India with doubts and hopes but her auntie's informal and extreme warm welcome has vanquished her easily and made her feel at home. Her aunt suggests if she wants to see "The real India the spiritual India" (UE-63) She accepts the proposal of pilgrimage in the hope that her own journey from US may bring her coveted change- a transformed self. In spite of her mother's advice not to "get involved in the lives of strangers" (UE61), she voluntarily gets involved in Mrs. Das who is lonely in a 'crowd' as in her own family as Leela is in her adapted home land. The company of Mrs. Das helps her to know the values of togetherness, the nuances of physical intimacy, and about being alone.

"The Love of Good Man' is a tale of happily married Indian woman- Monisha and Dilip and their son Bijoy. Her estranged father begs to meet his only grandson. Monisha knows his father was the only cause of her mother's death. Her mother used to tell her many wise sayings on different occasions at Calcutta before her marriage- *The love of good man saves your life, Anger is greater destroyer, Out of the bluest skies lightening strikes…etc.* She realized the meanings of these saying in the passage of time. Her husband Dilip's care, love and considerateness in the unknown land support her to handle emotional traumas and she realized the saying of her mother – *The love of good man saves your life*. Her father is culprit in her eyes who never deserves to be forgiven. But when she finds her father as helpless child her motherhood is evoked. She switches off the lamp and closes the door. She has developed some saying from her experience:

> I think I will start collecting saying of my own, invisible flowers spread greater fragrance. Home is where you move fluently through the dark. (UE-117)

The end of the story depicts transformation in Monisha – from hatred to forgiveness.

The 'Good Man' Umesh in the story, "What The Body Knows", takes care of his wife Aparna during her pregnancy and illness for a long time. In India we find husband rather hesitant in extending help to their wives but in Divakaruni's stories husbands are consciously liberated. In Indian gender hierarchy these family values are rather diminishing due to hesitations and pressures of society. In US these immigrants are creating new models of family where gender liberation is there in true sense. They have not succumbed to the pressures of US- their concept of individualism, privacy. Divakaruni's protagonists are both trapped and liberated by cultural changes in US. Aparana is emotionally infatuated with Dr. Byron who has saved her life. Aparna wants to tell him, "that he will always be unique in her life, the man who opened her up and touched the innermost cervices of her body who traveled with her Orpheus-like, the dusky alleyway between life and death" (UE- PP. 141-142). Her love for family is so powerful that she surpasses the emotional infatuation by refusing him; with apology when he asked for coffee. She drops his card into a garbage can and remembers her happy married life:

> Only an image: a hillside brown as a lion's skin, her husband running with a spool, her son yelling his excitement as she releases the kite. The fabric unfurling above them into the brief, vivid shape of human joy. (UE-143)

Jeff Zaleski writes about the various themes in the short story collection, *The Unknown Error of lives:*

Divakaruni writes intensely touching tales of lapsed communication, inarticulate love and redemptive memories. This is a mixed collection, then but one worth reading for the predominance of narratives that ring true as they illuminate the difficult adjustments of women in whom memory and duty must coexist with a new, often painful and disorienting set of standards.

Divakaruni's first novel *The Mistress of Spices* (1997), blends the immediacy of urban America-in this case Oakland, California- with the timeless mythology of ancient India. After her youngest son was born, she had a near death experience. *The Mistress of Spices* is the outcome of her near death experience. When she recovered from the serious complications, she felt strongly that she had returned for a purpose. She says of the experience:

> It was very positive, actually and it gave me the sense that we are here in this body only for a little while, and then we go on to other existences and may be other worlds that we don't know, and wanted to write about this, fictionalize it in some way (13)

This near-death experience made her realize, that we all have many lives and many identities and we move from one to another. This experience was so poignant that she wanted to bring in, the realm at the supernatural or magic in the fiction. She says:

> It was very important for me to try and work that into my writing, but I didn't know how to for a long time, until I began to have these very strong mental images of this old woman in an Indian grocery who had many lives and who would perhaps go on to have many more". (14)

In *The Mistress of Spices* Divakaruni presents, the central character, Tilo, an immigrant woman from a faraway land from India, who runs a spice shop in California. She sells *masalas* and gives free advice to the local Indian expatriate community. Each individual who comes to her is given different spices according to their problem, for *e.g.* cinnamon for strength, ginger for courage… . Upon taking her vows as a Mistress of spices, Tilo, is granted immortality on several conditions, one being that she must never succumb to carnal desires. The other important thing is that Mistress should not involve herself in other's problem. She should leave it to spices. The first mother Mistress says:

> Ultimately the mistresses are without power hollow reeds only for the wind's singing. It is the spice that decides and the person to whom it is given you must accept what they together choose and even with failure be at peace. (MS 139)

Emerging from a ritual fire, Tilo is transformed in to an old, ugly woman. Tilo, is gifted with supernatural power. She can see into to minds and hearts of her customers. Though Tilo has the supernatural power to foretell disasters, recommend spices, which can help immigrants to surmount their sorrows and fulfill their hopes; some times the problems of diaspora are too complicated that she cannot deal with it. Through the elaborate metaphor determined by spices, Divakaruni shows how it is possible for the individual to succeed in what she calls "dissolving boundaries" a necessity in the immigrant encounters. Every spice has medical remedy. Commenting on the uses of *'til'* and meaning of 'tillotama' she says:

> Till is the seasame seed under the sway of planet venus, gold brown as though just touched by flame. The flower of which is so small and straight and pointed that mothers pray for their girl child to have noses shaped like it. Til which ground into paste with sandalwood cures diseases of heart and liver, *til* which fried in its own oil restores luster when one has lost interest in life. I will be Tilottama, the essence of til, life giver, restorer of health and hope. (MS-42)

Tilo has re-created a little India in her store, she says of her store' "I think I do not exaggerate when I say there is no other place in the world quite like this. (MS-3) This store attracts a large group of people for whom the place is reminiscent of home, a little oasis in their diasporic lives full of problems. Tilo feels that the Indians come to her store in quest of happiness and to establish the connection with their homeland:

> All those voices, Hindi, Oriya, Assamese, Urdu, Tamil, English, layered one on the other like notes from a *tanpura* all those voices asking for more than their words, asking for happiness except no one seems to know where. (MS-78)

But the problem with Mistress is that she speaks hesitantly when a lonely American comes to her store and she cannot help him. She can easily communicate with Indians but not with the Americans she encounters – a situation that becomes a comment on the limitations of the intercultural transactions.

Though Tilo is unable to communicate with Americans, she is warned by the First Mother "The Others, they must go elsewhere. For their need" (MS-68). The mistress is allowed to use her power of magic for the good of her own people-that is Indians. Debjani Banerjee has rightly observed – how even within the structure of fable, Divakaruni has underscored the opaque nature of national borders. She writes:

> National Boundaries become aggressive, all important in the diaspora, as a way of defining identity, a liminality that marks the contours of one's experience, a platform for resisting co-optation by the dominant/hegemonic discourse. The store with its sacred, secret shelves functions as a geographical/textual space that is the repository of a monolithic national identity. (15)

The store represents a space for self indulgence "dangerous for a brown people who come from elsewhere, to whom real Americans might say *why*? (MS-5)

Before writing this novel, Divakaruni, conducted lot of research on the Internet and in the library. She talked informally with people in Indian groceries and collected the experiences from her help line "Maitri". Her own experience also helped her to express the feeling of loneliness and cultural separation that are within *The Mistress of Spices*. She was interested in showing the relationship between different cultures of colour in America and how in some ways we need each other. There should be a listening ear to share our experience and Tilo is doing this role in *The Mistress of Spices*. Regarding the importance of spices and the role of women, Divakaruni says:

> Spices are very ordinary every day things. They are very domestic; it is the woman who deals with the spices. And yet there is lot of power in the spices. They have herbal qualities; they have medicinal qualities; they have mythical qualities. These little things like the spices that we think of a domestic, if we use them right can have lot of power. (16)

The Mistress of Spices tries to capture the nuances that contest the stereotypical images of South Asian as model minorities and unobtrusive citizens. In the continuum with the title, each chapter is named after a spice and discusses the trials and tribulations of an individual and the special characteristics of the spices. Thus, the reader gets a glimpse into a range of problems that surround the life of the diasporic Indian. Mrs. Ahuja's is a story of dispossession. She left the settled, comfortable life at her father's house when she was married to a violent man, an alcoholic, who abuses her. She wants to start again in America. She says:

> Here in America may be we could start again, away from those eyes, those mouths always telling us how a man should act, what is a woman's duty. But ah the voices, we carried them all the way inside our heads. (MS. P. 102-103)

The mistress helps Mrs. Ahuja with special spice- 'fennel' which is the spice for Wednesdays. Tilo assures Mrs. Ahuja about the effect of 'fennel':

> It is a wondrous spice. Take a pinch of it, raw and whole, after every meal to freshen the breath and aid digestion and give you mental strength for what must be done... Give some to yours husband as well...Fennel cools the temper as well (MS-104)

The spices helped Mrs. Ahuja to become Lalita by over throwing the tyrannical structure that has weighed her down. Lalita leaves her husband and seeks refuge at a battered women's shelter. It was quite easy to take this step in America. For Geeta, Tilo mixes several ingredients, 'ginger' for deeper courage, 'fenugreek' for healing breaks and '*amchur*' for deciding right things. Geeta's predicament stems from the fact that she is part of a paradigmatic diasporic family where a clash between the first generation and second generation South Asian is inevitable. Her parents have 'given' plenty of independence but they cannot accept her boy friend. Geeta, the second generation American is not prepared for this volteface; she is shocked by the elements of racism that she perceives in her parents reaction to Juan. Geeta's grandfather was sure that the 'freedom' Geeta's father gave her, will spoil her:

> But mental peace I am not having, not even one iota, since I crossed the *kalapani* and came to this America...But I tell you better to have no granddaughter than one like this Geeta. May be Ok for all these *firingi* women in this country ...chee, chee, back in Jamshedpur they would have smeared dung on our faces for that. And who would ever marry her. But when I tell Ramu (Geeta's father), he says *Baba* don't worry they are only friends. (MS-85)

For the second generation Indian like Geeta, the question about identity is differently poised. She challenges continuous identification with patriarchal traditions, which she associates with her grandfather. Geeta's decision to marry Juan shattered entire family. Her mother is "crying and wringing her hands, saying I never thought you would do this to us, is this how you repay us for giving you so much freedom even though all our relatives warned us not to.... Dad, Geeta says, Dad. She shakes his arm, say something. He jerks away like he is getting electric shock. (MS-89-90).

Her grandfather declares, "Do what you like. Your father and I will think we were childless" (MS-90) Geeta declared, "very well". I am going to move in with Juan then. He is been asking me for a long time. I said no, thinking of you guys all this time, but now I will" (MS-90). Tilo, tries to assuage the pain of Geeta's family and succeeds in restoring harmony within family by suggesting them some spices:

> I pound him a powder of almond and *kesar* to boil in milk. The whole family must drink it at bedtime I say. To sweeten your words and thoughts, to remember the love buried under the anger. And you *dadu* who made much of this tangle, take special care what you say. No more talk of going back to India. When bitterness boils up in your mouth, wanting out, swallow it down with a spoon of this *draksha* syrup. (MS 91)

Tilo tries to cool down Geeta, "your grandfather loves you a lot" (MS-134). She tried 'to stop the poison eating at her heart'. (MS-134-135).

Divakaruni shows the difference between the first generation and the second generation-Indian Americans through Geeta's reaction to the 'love' of her grandfather:

'Love, hah'. She spits out the sound like a sickness. He doesn't know what the word means. For him it's all control. Control my parents, control me. And whenever he doesn't get his way it's *Ramu send me back better I die alone in India'*. (MS-135)

Geeta is so confused and depressed that though she is taking pills every night, she can't sleep. She decided to stay with her best friend Diana instead of Juan. She retains her Indian culture and never stays with Juan before marriage. She lives her contact number to Tilo, in case her family asks about her. She says to Tilo:

> May be you could show them this, you know; if they come to store or something, and you could maybe tell them also we're not living together. (MS-137)

The chapter 'Asafoetida', presents the story of Indian woman- who is overburdened by household work and her job. Daksha works as a nurse in US and when she comes home, she has to cook in Indian way, serve her husband, mother-in-law,. Day by day, it becomes difficult for Daksha to perform these double duties: she wants to tell her family that she is unable to work at home but she can't tell them. Tilo, suggests her spices which would help her to say ' NO':

> Daksha here is seed of black pepper to be boiled whole and drunk to loosen your throat so you can learn to say No, that word so hard for Indian women. *No* and *hear me now.* (MS-8)

Tilo, also suggest *Amla* for a different resistance and to bear unending pain. Tilo, tries to solve the problem of diasporic people but some time she can't solve as they are more complex. She cannot protect Mohan from racist attack on his store, which leaves him crippled, emotionally and physically. Jaggi is estranged and racially marked. A timid child; he is assaulted at school for not knowing English, for not belonging. In the play ground they try to pull it off his turban. They dangle the cloth from their fingertips and laugh at his long, uncut hairs and push him down. This worst experience has made Jaggi- a gangster, drug-supplier. Tilo, can't stop Jaggi- to becoming *lofar, gunda*. Her spices never stop him ruining: Tilo becomes restless:

> Inside me thought whirl like dust-devils. I can't breathe. O cinnamon strength-giver. Cinnamon friend-maker, what we have done. I clasp my fingers to stop the shaking Clove and cardamon that I scattered on wind for compassion, how did this happen. (MS-121)

Jaggi has developed haterate for "Indianless' because his 'Indianness' has made him 'odd' earlier in school life. Tilo wants to try some other spices so that she will get her innocent Jaggi back. But Jaggi refused: "Shit I don't need no smelly Indian tonic". Tilo never understand the reason behind the drastic change in Jagjit. She tries to analyze:

> And I left alone to walk stiffy back to the counter, to lower my aching head into my hands, to wonder in dismay what went wrong. To ask myself over and over, was it him? Was it his parents, was it America? (MS-122)

The novel shows some immigrants create their won space in America, some assimilates and prospers economically and some lose their jobs or worse, their children.

There is a feminist voice and strong female characters in *The Mistress of Spices* and Divakaruni's following fiction. This is important on going theme in her stories because she is influenced by the community work that she is doing for many years with battered women. According to Divakaruni, women should have choices and life of dignity. They should take their own domestic space and empower it. The mistress- the deliberate gendering of the word to undercut the power associated with mastery is to be noted has supernatural powers. Only in her hands "the spices sang back" (MS-34). Selvan Veena comments on Chitra Banerjee and her feminist voice in her fiction:

> Chitra Banerjee Divakaruni is a product of the postmodern spirit. Her fundamental preoccupation, revealed in her two novels *The Mistress of Spices* and *Sister of My Hearts,* is to create a female universe out of (though not out side of) the conventional male world. The male universe is not altogether shut out. There is the obvious effort to bridge the two. But there is a definite attempt at defining them as distinctive domains. (17)

In *The Mistress of Spices,* Divakaruni rejects the conventional geography. Tilo, the protagonist, learns to be a mistress on a far away island that cannot be located on a regular globe:

> The island has been there forever, said the snakes, the old one also. Even we who saw the mountains grow from buds of rock on the ocean bed, who were there when Samudra Puri, the perfect city, sank in the aftermath of the great flood, do not know there beginning... The island...what does it look like? And she? (MS-23)

It is significant that female universe is an island. It is cut of from the male universe. The mistresses can establish the connection with human world only when the mistress of their own volition reaches out to the other world: Tilo says:

> ... When I woke in this land the store was already around me, its hard, protective shell. The species too surrounded me, a shell of smells and voices. And that other shell, my aged body pressing its wrinkles into me. Shell within shell, and inmost of all my heart beating like a bird (MS-125)

Tilo, can retain her supernatural power provided she has to suppress her personal desire. Tilo, is not permitted to leave shop. Men may enter it but do not belong there. The order of Mistresses clearly replicates patriarchal structures and Tilo breaks this to live her own life. Tilo, falls in love with handsome American Raven and decides to transform into a young woman to fulfill her desires. Though she feels guilty about her "Self indulgence", she decides to face the retribution that she should have to face (MS-173). She is in dilemma whether to be selfless or selfish. If she experienced the pleasure of human being, she will loose her supernatural power. She has to leave domain, the beautiful, organized spice store, in order to fulfill individual desire. However the novel validates women's empowerment through articulation of their desires. At the end of the novel Tilo becomes Maya, the young woman who has abandoned her special powers. She says, "I who now have only myself to hold me up" (MS-317). She found her new identity new home through an act of cultural translation. The success of *The Mistress of Spices* has kept Divakaruni hop-scorching across the country, as well as to England and back to her native India. The husband of Gurinder Chadha has directed movie on this novel in which Ashwarya Roy is doing the role of main heroine. Commenting on the novel Divakaruni says:

> Women in particular respond to my work because I am writing about them – women in love, in difficulties, women in relationships. I want people to relate to my characters to feel their joy and pain, because it will be harder to (be) prejudiced when they meet them in real life, (18)

Sister of My Heart (1999) is the second novel by Chitra Banerjee, which extends a story, 'The Ultrasound' from the short story collection *Arranged Marriage. The Vine of Desire,*

Published in 2002 is the sequel of *Sister of My Heart*. "The Ultrasound" is a story about two women Anju and Arundhati who are cousins, who grew up in a middle urban context. Anju lives in America and so she has access to a variety of technological and other kind of advantages. But at the same time she questions her position as a wife in a certain kind of patriarchal framework. Her cousin Arundhati who remains in India has married into a very conservative family. And when ultrasound reveals that her child is going to be a girl, they want to get it aborted. Arundhati left her home alone with jewelry. In her interview with Sarah Anne Johnson, Chitra Banerjee was talking about the whole process of writing *Sister of My Heart* and *The Vine of Desire*. When "The Ultrasound" was done, she says:

> I wanted to go back and examine the beginning of these characters' lives. I became very interested in how they thought and under what circumstances would they have grown up to lead them that moment of story in *Arranged Marriage*. (19)

In this way she wrote *Sister of My Heart*. In the novel, two women, cousins-Anju and Sudha were told that they were born after their fathers died in pursuit of rubies. Anju and Sudha, distant cousins born on the same day, form a bond of sisterhood that no one quite understand and match. Divakaruni wrote a chapter in Anju's voice and a Sudh's voice, alternatively which helped a smooth development of the story. They feel the narratives of their lives and relationships. They grow up together, carefree and sheltered by their mothers (Gouri and Nalini and Gauri's widowed sister-in-law, Pishi) and an array of servants in a massive crumbling old house. Anju is witty, intelligent daughter of Gouri Ma, a proud descendent of the wealthy Chaterjee family. She grows with many dreams including higher education. Sudha was rather homely, beautiful and comes from the branch of the family tree that is shadowy and dark. Her dream is to become a perfect wife and mother.

Life was not always the bed of roses for these two women. When Pishi told a dark family secret to Sudha that her father has murdered Anju's father, both her perception of herself and her connection to Anju falters slightly. Sudha was fallen in love with Ashok who was from the lower caste. For the sake of Anju she accepts arranged marriage. The girls were not only born on same day, but are set to be wedded on the same day- in marriages arranged by Mothers and years later become pregnant simultaneously – Anju lives in America and Sudha stayed behind in India.

Before their marriage they were happy in a female universe. The girl live in a matriarchal home in which there is no male control. The only male alive in the family is disguised as Singhji, the driver and exerts no authority over the household. After marriage, both Sudha and Anju's life is changed. Marriage tears them part- Anju moves to America and Sudha to rural Bengal. Men separate them effectively in terms of geography. Their lives are shattered when they attempt to conform to the rules of the masculine society. Anju almost loses her mental stability after the miscarriage of baby and Sudha her freedom. When Sudha's mother-in-law discovers, she is expecting a girl she wants to get it, aborted. Sudha refuses and is divorced. Ashok is ready to marry Sudha but Sudha decided to go to America for the sake of Anju. Only female bond can solve their problem. Anju couldn't control her joy, excitement at the arrival of Sudha:

> Sudha's coming, Sudha's coming! She'll be here in a week! I am buffeted between joy and panic – there's so much to be done to get the apartment ready before she arrives. I hadn't expected the visa to come through so fast. I suspect it's because Sunil went to my doctor and made him write a letter about how Sudha's getting here is crucial to my recovery. And of course it is. Not just getting here, but her staying her. The visa is only valid for a year, but I have heard those things can be arranged. Maybe Sudha can go to college here. May be we will get that business started. Maybe she will meet someone who'll make up for what she's giving up to come here. (SH-318)

It is only beyond the male world that the protagonists find safety. Female bonding is definitely different form male bonding. Sudha and Anju need bond with one another (even after their marriages) to create a safe refuge for themselves. Divakaruni talks about her ideas about female bonding in her article for *Bold Type:*

> In the best friendship ....with women, there is a closeness that is unique, a sympathy that comes from somewhere deep and prinal in our bodies and does not need explanation, perhaps because of the life, changing experiences we share menstruation, child birth, menopause. The same tragedies, physical or emotional, threaten us... We take joy in the same small good things of life Oh, we fight too. We are sometimes furiously competitive and bitchy and exasperated. But ultimately we can be our selves with each other. Ourselves with all our imperfections. Ourselves uncomplicated by all the emotions that complicate our other relationships; duty, lust, romance the need to impress or control. We can be women and that, as women, we are understood. (20)

In both her novels – including *The Mistress of Spices* the idea of female bonding is explored. But there is a greater focus on this theme in *Sister of My Heart*. Divakaruni comments on the theme of *Sister of My Heart:*

> My latest novel *Sister of My Heart* explores the particular nature of women's friendships, what makes them special and different. The two main characters, Sudha and Anju, grow up in the same household, love each other fiercely and completely, and know each other so well that they believe no one else will ever know them this way. (21)

In the novel *Sister of My Heart,* the bond between two protagonists, Anju and Sudha is examined. The title itself brings out the emotional ties between the two women. Divakaruni's use of the word "sister" in both her novels *The Mistress of Spices* and *Sister of My Heart* reflects her specific concern. "Sister" here is used in the sense of a universal sisterhood, a female universe by itself. Sudha and Anju live in a world of their own removed from the others around them. Anju says:

> I could never hate Sudha. Because she is my other half. The sister of my heart. I can tell Sudha everything I feel and not have to explain any of it. She'll look at me with those big unblinking eyes and smile a tiny smile, and I know she understands me perfectly. (SH-24)

Divakaruni has declared that 'sisterhood' is her theme of writing. She clearly put the theme in the context of the Western tradition rather than of India Her fiction deals with the problems of the first and second-generation Asian immigrant women. They are constantly struggling to assimilate and to keep their ethnic identity alive. Urbashi Barat comments on the theme of female bonding in Asian American women writing:

> For Asian or African American women, sisterhood is a strength and succours, enabling them to discover themselves as persons and to nurture their ties with their community; friendship with other women becomes, therefore central to the fiction of all American "Women of color". (22)

Being an immigrant, Divakaruni has the experience of the trauma of unassimilation, terrible isolation. Friendship with women has given a way to her emotions and helped her to reconstruct her identity in a new world. So "sisterhood" has been an inevitable theme of her fiction. Almost all her fiction centres around Indian immigrant women and their uneasy relationship with unfamiliar world. Urbashi Barat has rightly pointed the conviction, run through Divakaruni's work and which is shared by most Asian American women writers:

> ....that it is only in this new world, in spite of all the pain and alienation it brings, in spite of the bitterness of the realization that the pot of gold at the end of at the rainbow might elude her forever, that she can find her selfhood and real sisterhood. (23)

The net-working among the immigrant women brings solace in their life.

Divakaruni challenges the male superiority and uses Anju- the more rebellious than Sudha, to demolish the Western myth of superiority and validity. In Anju, Divakaruni presents the cultural bias of the colonized hybrid. Anju constantly interrogates the validity of the native culture. She was fascinated by the western literature. Virginia Woolf's novel – *A Room of One's Own*, becomes a prized possession. She records her feelings for the book:

> Woolf has been a favourite of mine since the time I stumbled upon one of her books at the store. It was beautiful, old, leather bound volume, printed in England, with an intriguing title, *A Room of One's Own*. When put my nose to thick pages, they smelled unlike Indian books with their rice glue binding. I thought of it as the smell of distance, of new thinking. That smell stayed with me a long time. It stood for something I wanted but didn't know a name for. (SH-134)

Anju loves Virginia Woolf. Sunil, her husband uses the knowledge of Woolf to woo Anju. She discovers in America, that he has fake knowledge of Woolf. His deception is the beginning of her disillusement with Western sophistication. Her misconception about the freedom dissolves when she migrated to America after marriage. She realizes that having short hair, wearing jeans and using expletives are not signs of emancipation. She couldn't cope with the challenges of the new world. It is only when Sudha narrates to her a story based on Indian mythology over the phone, Anju recovers and her wilting spirit is re-energized. Though *Sister of My Heart* and *The Vine of Desire* depend less on magical realism, there is the element of fairy tale. Sudha is gifted with the power to invent stories based on Pishi's mythological narrations. Pishi used to tell about the princes who is locked away forever in her mother-in-law's fortress, waiting to be rescued. There is the brave warrior queen who defends herself and her baby against an army who are trying to harm her. But when Sudha narrates the story to Anju in America, she reinterprets this myth and the princes instead of waiting for the prince to save her, finds courage to flee from the prison and find asylum with a woman. C. N. Eswari comments on Anju's recovery from depression after listening the tale told by Sudha:

> By rewriting Sudha's favourite tale Divakaruni tacitly undermines the notion of men being the preserver of women. Simultaneously the folklore acts as a sustaining mechanism for Anju who is floundering in an alien environment and serves to encode the novels message that for a rootless immigrant the native tradition provides the much needed anchorage. (24)

Divakaruni has reflected through her fiction that our tradition and myths have helped Indian immigrants to establish their roots in an alien land.

Anju invites Sudha to start a new life in America, no matter what it cost to her, financially and emotionally. Since Sunil connot afford Sudha's fare, she herself takes up a job, overworks and loses her baby. Sudha arrives in America with her daughter to join Anju and together decide to bring up the child. Coming together does not resolve their individual problem. Sudha knows that her presence in Anju's marriage will inevitably cause problems and unhappiness, something that Sudha had anticipated long before in an old dream:

> If only Anju and I like the wives of the heroes in the old tales, could marry the same man, our Arjun, our Krishna, who would love and treasure us both, and keep us both together. (SH-123)

Though Anju was clever, but she was less imaginative and more sensitive. She has always stood by Sudha. She is ready to sacrifice her relationship with Sunil to help Sudha finding her own space in America. The novel ends with Anju's thoughts:

> We have formed a tableau, two women, their arms intertwined, their arms entwined like lotus stalks smiling down at the baby between them. Two women who have travelled the vale of sorrow and the baby who will save them, who has saved them already. Madonna's with child...

> for now the three of us stand unhurried, feeling the way we fit, skin on skin, into each other's lives. A rain-dampened sun struggles from the clouds to frame us in its hesitant holy light. (SH-347)

By synthesizing these two contradictory yet complementary characters, Divakaruni succeeds in presenting the new identity of the immigrant who validates the cultural past to reconstruct a meaningful present in the new world. Thus the novel ends not with the celebration of assimilation but with creation of a new identity and a new home. Sudha and Anju's coming together, help in recharging their energy to face life anew.

C. N. Eswari has studied *Sister of My Heart* as post colonial feminist work. He writes:

> Chitra Banerjee Divakaruni's *Sister of My Heart* may rightly be regarded as a post colonial feminist writing by an immigrant writer who has prolonged her post-colonial status through voluntary migration – as an inferior "other" under colonial hegemony: as a subordinate sex in a male dominated society; and as a racial minority in her new home. Yet she rises above these social limitations to relate "her-story" that at once enables her to reconstruct her values, culture and history and frees her from labels and categories that dominant groups have placed on her experience and identity. (25)

Divakaruni's lyrical language allows her readers to imagine the atmosphere of characters lives and to feel their joy, disappointment, sisterhood and sorrow. Though these are not Divakaruni's stories but she has interest in these issues. She is completely involved in these characters and their struggle. Throughout *The Vine of Desire* characters tell fairy tales. While explaining the power of fairy tale in a person's life, Divakaruni says:

> The fact is that these tales have been very interesting and important to me and I have often thought about how we relate our modern lives to these tales. What is that, is archetypal in these tales that still calls us? Not just the

tales out of my culture but mythic tales from every culture – have such a hold on the human imagination, because in some ways they are reflecting certain realities that come up over and over in our lives. (26)

These fairy tales reflect the harsh reality of our life and we get the solution of many problems. These fairy tales help us to understand the patterns of our life. Divakaruni encounters a new meaning regarding desire in western context where desire is positive and is related to goal-getters. This new meaning of desire is resulted in. *The Vine of Desire* (Feb-2002) a sequel of *Sister of My Heart.* In *The Vine of Desire,* Divakaruni takes up the story of Anju and Sudha where she left them at the end of her novel – *Sister of My Heart.* After escaping the tyrannical grip of her mother-in-law in India, Sudha and her infant daughter, Dayita have come to live with Anju and Sunil in San Francisco. Anju had to face the consequences of this decision to invite Sudha to their place. Anju must learn to cope with the loss of her unborn child, her husband's emotional rejection, and overcome a deep sense of betrayal by Sudha. When Sunil used to see restless depressed Anju, he says, "I don't know how to help you when you are like this" (VD-10) Anju used to replied, "you don't need to do anything". (VD-11). It is generally observed – husband never understand his wife when she is depressed or husband never wants to understand his wife. Anju becomes speechless. She needs a emotional support. In her interior-monologue she says:

Inside her head she added, except love me. Inside her head he replied, I do love you. Inside her head she said, But not enough. (VD-11)

Anju discovers that her husband Sunil, harbours passion for Sudha and Sudha also loves him. Her soulmate become her rival. In *Sister of My Heart* they had a sense that they could be everything to each other, and in *The Vine of Desire* they realize that they can't. They have lost the early innocence. They had become more complicated as they grew up in a different environment. As they never fulfilled some of their earlier dreams, they have become darker characters. In *The Vine of Desire* they have to go forward and deal with tragedies, disappointment and betrayals. They come together in a alien land, their motives were good but the consequence of their decision to have their own space, was not in their hand. They can't forgive each other. They realize the fact that you can love someone even when they can't be everything to you and even when they let you down.

It was very difficult for Anju to come out of this painful journey, because her sense of value as a woman is tied up with her success as a wife and mother. She wrote a letter to her mother:

Santa Clara

September 1994

Dear Mother,

I read in your letter about Sunil's father's death. I can't pretend to be sorry...

What I am about to write will be as a shock to you ......Sunil and I have separated. He wants a divorce. He told me he loves Sudha, has loved her a long time. He's gone to Houston with a new assignment; I am staying in a nearby city with a friend, a woman I met at the university, who took me in when I was at the end of my rope.

.... Sudha has taken up a job, I think I have not seen her, don't wish to. She left suddenly without explanation...... My life feels like there is a gaping hole at the center of it. I tiptoe around it. One misstep and I will plunge in.

I can't write any more now. But mostly, I want you not to worry. I was worse before. I wanted to hurt myself. Now I have decided otherwise. I want to show them that I can survive in spite of what they have done to me

Yours daughter

Anju (VD-269-70)

Anju started taking interest in the creative writing assignments and extra curricular activities of college. She sheds her old value system and takes steps towards living a new life. In her last meeting with Sudha , she says "I have learned to fly" (VD-368).

Sudha never had the luxuries like Anju. She has to provide shelter and food for her daughter, working around the clock for a bitter octogenarian Indian man Mr. Sen. However her work and new-found connection with the octogenarian prove to be a way (route) for Sudha in this unknown land. She felt herself guilty. She realizes that even though she can choose to wear a sari or blue jeans and a t-shirt in her world, she'll only ever feel a sense of belonging when she returns to India. Sudha wrote to Anju, Sunil, Pishi, Ashok about her decision to go back to India. She was not sure whether Anju will forgive her or not. The only thing Sudha was proud of – she writes to her aunt Pishi, "But think of this: for the first time in my life, I will have my own bank account. It makes me feel – finally like a grown up! (VD-350) Her aunt Pishi consoles her through a letter:

> Don't worry about Anju's anger. Whether she wants to or not, she can't hate you. You are too much part of each other. Can the left hand hate the right? (VD-351)

Jeff Zaleski writes about the challenges faced by the protagonists in *The Vine of Desire*:

> This exquisitely rendered tale of passion, jealousy and redemption continues the extraordinary relationship between Anju and Sudha, the two exceptional women at the heart of Divakaruni's praised *Sister of My Heart*. The two cousins have traveled a lifetime away from their home city of Calcutta to California, a place so foreign to their native culture and traditions that must they have constantly re-evaluated their bearings and values..... Divakaruni expertly juxtaposes the challenges, freedoms and crassness of modern...day America with the issues, both personal and cultural, each woman faces. (27)

Divakaruni's Sixth novel *Queen of Dreams* (2004) is a pleasantly a typical tale of self-discovery. Leaving one's homeland for distant, unknown shores is at ones pain and pleasure. Divakaruni reveals:

> It is the pain of leaving the homeland but also the excitement of being in a new place – that is the duality of immigration. Now there is another exciting movement – the second generation trying to connect back with the homeland? (28)

Earlier this Overseas Born Indians were called as ABCD (American Born Confused Desi). They are AB but no longer CD. Born to Indian parents, OBIS are not the citizens of India. Though their parents lived in the US for many years still they regard India as their home. Second generation Indians are essentials foreigners with varying degrees of Indians influence, whereas first-generation Indians are Indians with varying degree of foreign influence. The connection of the second generation Indian American to their homeland – is a major theme of *Queen of Dreams.*

The novel opens by plunging the reader into middle of a character's dream. The character whose dream reader shares is Mrs. Gupta, a first generation Indian immigrant to America, she is the queen of dreams. Her 'work' consists of reading other people's dreams and warning them of future. Mrs. Gupta's daughter Rakhi – is the other protagonist of the story. Rakhi is a young, second generation Indian American immigrant. She is an artist and single mother in Berkeley, California. She has a strong connection to her 'Indian-ness' and cannot understand why her mother refuses to speak of India. Though she is an artist, she has to run a tea-shop named *"The Chai House"* to earn a living and to look after her six year old daughter, Jona, a third generation Indian American. A trouble soon appears in the shape of rival coffee shop. Her customers begin to transfer to her lower priced competitor. If Rakhee is unable to support Jona fincancially, she may lose the custody of her six year old daughter to ex-husband, Sonny.

Meanwhile Rakhi receives the welcome news that her work is accepted for display of a prestigious art gallery. Unfortunately, while returning from the art gallery Rakhi's parents were involved in a car accident. Her mother died on spot and father was injured. Her mother's death is a turning point in the novel. Before her mother's death her father was very kind, gentle and insignificant. But after the death of Mrs. Gupta, he emerged as a star. His talents as cook, singer help to run *"The Chai House"* back on its feet. Rakhee, longs to know more about her mother's past and Indian heritage. Rakhi with her father's help started reading the journals that Mrs. Gupta left behind for her husband and child.

Divakaruni's earlier novel, short stories explore the rich and complex relationships between women but in *Queen of Dreams,* daughter-father relationship is highlighted. Without her father Rakhi cannot open the secrets of her mother's journals. Commenting on the father daughter relationship, Divakaruni writes:

> As with much of my work, it isn't that I set out to do this, it's just where the story evolved organically. The mother is mystery to the daughter from the beginning and it's only after she dies that her words come to the daughter through the journals, but they have to be translated by the father. More than the male or female relationship I think what I was looking at was how in leaving our home culture we lose a lot of it and often we need help. We need translators [29]

Everything was going normal and the national tragedy – 9/11 happens. Her life is shaken by new horrors. The same day, two white man attacked Rakhee, her friends and her family out the *"The Chai House"* In the wake of September 11, she and her friends must deal with dark new complexities about their acculturation. Rakhi's feelings about being treated as hostile, alien are poignantly delineated: "But if I wasn't Americans then what was I?" (QD-301)

After – 9/11, Indian-American's were looked 'suspicious'. One day Rakhi found that someone had painted 'TERRORIST' in red letters over the name of their store. Her ex-husband, Sonny brings copies of e-mails that are being circulated by Indian organizations. The notes caution them:

> ... not to go anywhere alone...Don't wear your native clothes (what native clothes? she wonders, looking down

> at her pants) put up American flags in prominent locations in homes and businesses (But this she cannot bring herself to do) Pray. When she listens to the president's military plans, she feels a need for prayer, but she doesn't know which deity, American or Indian, she should aim her supplications. Who should be forgiven, and who saved. (QD 304-05)

Rakhi couldn't bear the suspicious glances on the street. People never walk beside her on the street. Rakhi wonders, "How is it that one can become, overnight, both so frightening, and so vulnerable? (QD P. 305). Some of the Americans feel sorry for the terrible attack on her. They want to welcome her presence in their community. They make her feel like a guest Rakhi was confused and shocked:

> I was born here, she wants to tell them. How can you welcome me? (QD-305)

Rakhi invites Sonny, cooks for him. There is warmth in her kitchen as she is with Jona and Sonny. She tells Sonny how her neighborhood has changed after – 9/11:

> The Pakistani women barely come out of their apartments. The Afghani men take turns rounding up the children of their community and driving them to the neighborhood school, although it is only two blocks away. (QD-306-307)

Divakaruni uses – 9/11 as a huge lever in the story. Divakaruni reveals the reason:

> What it did for me as an individual was to bring up the questions that Rakhi has to face: If I am not American, or if people don't see me as American, then what does that do to my identity? (30)

Divakaruni does a good job by working on current issues into a novel and avoids synthetic characterization.

In this novel she tried to bring out the problem of identity. How can diaspora live in the country where they are considered as terrorists? How can they continue to live in America as Americans? Her basic purpose of writing is emphasizing similarities in different ethnic groups rather than differences. In the novel *Queen of Dreams,* she tried to mix the dream world and the world of painful realities. She reveals the purpose behind it:

> I wanted to point to the complexity of human experience and then the whole mysterious level of what is real and what isn't. Sometimes what is 'real' because it takes place in the physical world, like 9/11, is so unreal on the level of the soul. Then other things, which in terms of the physical world seem so magical and unbelievable, on the level of the soul, seem very real. I hope that worked for the reader. (31)

September-11 disrupts Rakhi's search for identity, and a vicious attack on her friends and family calls their notions of citizenship into question.

Divakaruni's has written her latest novel *The Palace of Illusions* from the perspective of Draupadi. Right from the childhood the aloneness of epic heroine strike strange to Divakaruni. As sisterhood is her major theme, she finds Indian epic inadequate. Remytholization of Indian epic became an important tool in her hand. She reinterprets the ancient Indian myths and epics and makes them blend with the story of immigrant Indian women struggling to assimilate in alien culture and at the same time struggling to keep alive the tradition, values and memories of the homeland. Though sisterhood is recurrent theme in her novel and short stories, she considers relationship with men equally important. In *Mistress of Spices, Queen of Dreams and Palace of Illusions,* husbands and lovers play significant roles. She is interested in creating a world where men and women are treated with equal respect and allowed choices.

This is the era of retelling epics. Tara publishers released Samhita's work, which is Sita's Ramayana- a graphic novel retelling epic from Sita's perspective. There are certain other names in the field of retelling epic – Ashok Banker, Amish Tripathi, Ashwin Sanghi and Gita Chandra. They write in such a way that they can relate to today's youngsters. While giving reason to the need of retelling epics Chitra Banerjee says:

"Myths and epics speak to the something deep and unchanging in the human soul and that's why we return to them again and again in an effort to solve the riddle of existence. Perhaps in times of rapid change, such as India is undergoing currently, we are particularly attracted to the timeless elements in Myths". (32)

Indian epics are becoming popular all over the world. India is doing well in almost all fields and it has gained confidence.

At this juncture entire world including India is eager to know about Indian epics. Chitra Banerjee tops the list to popular feminist retelling of Indian epics. The novel *Palace of Illusion* is different because of Draupadi's story. The novel is written in the first person. Draupadi recounts the epic from the time she and her brother Drishtadyumna are born out of the sacrificial fire and adopted by king Drupad. In this novel Divakaruni has adopted a very simple, lucid prose style. Draupadi through her words conversation carefully unfolds the different layers of the *Mahabharata*. Divakaruni's Draupadi is in many ways different and modern a woman retelling against the fact that the major decisions in her life are taken by men without taking her into consideration. Divakaruni through this novel highlights the vital truth that strong women tend to have unhappy marriages be they Kunti, Draupadi and Gandhari.

Neela: Victory Song (Sept. 2002) is Divakaruni's first children book. It is a historical fiction for youth. It follows the story of twelve- years old girl caught up in the Independence movement. Instead of getting married to a wealthy and cultural family she plunged into a Independence movement. She disguises herself as a boy and face many adventures. In this novel Divakaruni juggles two difficult goals: presenting the story of Indian independence and presenting it as a 12 years old girl might have seen it. Reader gains a new understanding of Asian history and culture. The experience and emotions of Neela are timeless and intense. This novel is included in '*Girls Many Land Series*' featuring books based on young girls from various historical periods and cultural traditions.

Another book Divakaruni wrote for the children is *The Conch Bearer* (2003). While giving reason behind writing this book for children, Divakaruni says:

> This book is very important for me. I started thinking about it right after 9/11 because I felt that we were living in a world where we really needed cross-cultural understanding in the paranoia and hate crimes that occurred across the nation right afterward. My community was affected, among many other communities. I wanted to do something to open children's minds to other cultures, because I was feeling that by the time people are adults, it's too late. (33)

As children's mind is much purer, they are more open-minded and innocent. They are eager to know the world around them. Especially these diaspora children are confused because of the native culture at home and western culture of their adopted home. Children are not aware of the terrorist's attack and its consequences. That's why Divakaruni decided to write books for children so that they can understand complexities of the world and they will develop cross cultural understanding.

Writing for children is very difficult task. One has to develop children's perspective and one has to understand the language of children. In her interview with Sarah A. J. Divakaruni agreed:

> I couldn't have written these two books without my two boys. They are 9 and 11 and they really helped me a lot. (34)

The personality of child is shaped by the kind of reading he does in his childhood. Now days *Harry Potter* is becoming very famous as the book is full of fantasy, magic realism and adventure. When Divakauni was growing up in Calcutta, she read a lot of Indian folk tales and fairy tales. She read our epics, *The Srimad Valmiki Ramayana* and *The Mahabharata.* She also heard a lot of oral tales from her mother. A lot of mythical ideas from Indian culture are woven into *The Conch Beaver*. In the novel whole concept of the conch is the magical object, an object of power.

The story opens in a poor section of Kolkatta, where 12 years old Anand is entrusted with a conch shell imbued with mystical powers. Anand's task is to return the shell to its rightful home high in the mountains. While Anand is at work one day at a tea stall in Kolkatta, he offers a beggar man his own ration of tea and '*pooris*' only to discover that the man is a healer, Abhayadatta, a mysterious man of indeterminate age wins Anand's and his mother's confidence by healing Anand's sister, who had stopped speaking after witnessing murder. Convinced by the old man's healing of he daughter, Anand's mother allows him to go on a journey with the stranger to return a magical conch shell to its rightful place in the Himalayas. Nisha a headstrong resourceful child of the street accompanies Anand in their journey, which is just like traditional good versus evil pilgrimage. This journey is full of fantansy, magic, adventures, spirituality and a fast trek from Kolkatta to a hidden paradise high in the Himalayas. Anand encounters, good and evil both in himself and in those around him. School children can enjoy this story with an unusual twist on the journey theme. During their journey they reach to valley of Brotherhood. Master Healer gave the conch of magic power to Anand and declares him to be caretaker of conch. Anand couldn't believe it but there was choice- whether he wanted to stay in the valley of Brotherhood and use the power of magic 'conch' for the welfare of people – or he wanted to go back to real world to stay with family? The chief Healer asked "can you make me forget, too?" (CB252) There was sorrow and firmness in the Healer's voice. The chief Healer says:

> Those of the Brotherhood must remember, no matter how much the pain. They must remember all that they sacrificed for the sake of becoming a Healer, for only then will they value what they learn here with every step they take into

> their new lives, they must realize that..." Anand heard his own voice completing the old man's sentence: ".....in order to gain something great, one must release his hold on something else equally beloved". (CB-252)

With the help of magic power of conch, Anand saw his family at dinner table and realized their routine life is in continuation. They are enjoying their life, planning for picnic. He realized his choice to stay in the valley of Brotherhood was right. The chief Healer said:

> We welcome you into the Brotherhood. You brought us back our hope and our power. Indeed, you brought back the life of the valley, and we thank you for that. Now you have chosen to give up much to be with us, and we appreciate that, too. It is my hope that you will find among your brother- and sister- Healers a family equally loving as the one you left and a home equally secure. May you learn much and heal many, and do your part to keep the valley safe, and world also. (CB 258).

Motivated by the tensions and crimes that flared after Sept.-11, specifically those aimed at her ethnic community, Divakaruni tried to emphasize the similarities among the people through the tale of 12 years old Indian boy – Anand. The feeling of brotherhood and sisterhood will definitely help diasporic communities to cope up with the consequences of the national tragedy of September 11.

Divakaruni has written Brotherhood of conch series. *Mirror of Fire and Dreaming (2005)* is the sequel of Conch Bearer. *Shadowland (2009)* is sequel of *Mirror of Fire and Dreaming*. Conch Bearer is set in contemporary India, while *Mirror of Fire and Dreaming* is set in several hundred years back in the past to the time of the Moghul rulers. In *Shadowland* the journey is in a future world. The magical adventure of The Brotherhood of The Conch Series has same characters, Anand and Nisha. In the *Mirror of Fire and Dreaming* Anand encounters powerful sorcerers, spoiled princes, nobel warriors and evil jinns. This book continues the adventures of Anand and his quest to become a full member of the Brotherhood of the conch. There he continues to learn the secret arts of the Brotherhood. In *Shadowland* his magical conch is stolen by an unknown force and suddenly his adopted home is reduced to a barren wasteland. Anand with friend Nisha embarks on dangerous mission-traveling to the cold and forbidding world of *Shadowland* in his attempt to restore the conch to its rightful place, and his home to its original splendor. Talking about the inspiration behind writing this "*Brotherhood Conch*" series Divakaruni says:

> I have always loved magical Indian tales I grew up with. I wanted to write a similar story that had Indian characters and an Indian setting and that used some of the elements of the Indian folk or fairy tale. I wanted such a story to be available for my sons as well as other children of different ethnic backgrounds in this country [US] for them to relate to and enjoy India character (35).

Divakaruni is actively engaged in the act of re-imagining space. In the act of reworking spatial parameters, Divakaruni has taken the first step towards defining new trajectories for the literature written by South Asians in the Indian Diaspora. Homi Bhabha describes the formulation of diasporic literature in *The Location of Culture:*

> What is....politically crucial is the need to think beyond narratives of imaginary and initial subjectivities and to focus on those moments or processes that are produced in the articulation of cultural differences. (36)

Divakaurni's writing focuses on those moments or processes that are produced in the articulation of cultural differences. Her fiction concentrates on portraying the quest for identity in the new spatial configurations while simultaneously trying to assimilate with the adopted home. Debjani Banerjee has rightly observed the way Divakaruni has created her own space as the South Asian American writer:

> The complex implications of working with cultural production in the west cannot be overemphasized. The possible complicity becomes a charged issue when we consider that amongst the many writers working in the

United States – and we see some powerful clippings of their work in anthologies – Divakaruni has attained considerable popularity and is sought after by the big publishing houses. This enhances the anxieties amongst critics and rightly so, as it points to the voices that are not being heard or celebrated with the same vigour. (37)

Divakaruni's texts are powerful and significant as they effectively map the contours of the new South Asian community in the United States and their struggle for identity.

REFERENCES

1. Banerjee Debjani, 'Home and US ': Re-defining Identity in the South Asian Diaspora through the Writings of Chitra Banerjee Divakaruni and Meena Alexander", *Diasporic Imagination Asian-American Writing* Vol-2. Fiction: Novels and short stories ed. by Somadatta Mandal. Pub. Prestige Books Ed. 2000. P.N.10.
2. Jaidka Manju, "The Writer as Trishanku: Indian Writing in a Foreign Space". *The Diasporic Imagination Asian American Writing.* Vol.3 Theory, poetry and the Performing Arts. ed. by Somadatta Mandal. Prestige 2002, p. 22.
3. Bhabha Homi, "Dissemination: Time, Narrative, and the Margins of the Modern Nation". *Nation and Narration.* ed. by Homi Bhabha Pub. London: Routledge, 1990, P.N.300
4. Sofky Elezabeth, "Cross-cultural Understanding Spiced with India Diaspora", *Black issues in Higher Education.* Reston: Sept 18, 1997. Vol.14.1ss, 15, p. 28
5. *Ibid.*, (p. 27)
6. Jussawalla Feroza, "Chiffon Saris: the Flight of Asian Immigrants in the New World." *Massachusetts Review*, 29, No. 4. (1998): p. 583.
7. Bhabha Homi, *op. cit.*, pp. 3-4
8. Banerjee Debjani, *op. cit.*, p. 15
9. Alexander, Meena, *The shock of Arrival: Reflections on Postocolonial Experience* Boston: South Press; 1996, p. 65.
10. Wong Salling C., "Middle-class Asian American in the Statue of Liberty in Divakaruni and Minatoya", *MELUS*, vol.29, Numbers 3&4. Fall/winter 2004, p. 196.
11. Sethi R.C.,"Arranged Marriage: stories," *Studies in short fiction.* Newberry: Spring 1996. Vol. 33, p. 287.

12. Zaleski Jeff, "The Unknown Errors of Lives," *Publishers Weekly*, New York: Mar.12, 2001, Vol. 248. p. 61.
13. Farmanfarmaian R, "Chitra Banerjee Divakaruni: Writing from a Different Place" *Publishers Weekly*. New York: May 14,2001. Vol. 248.
14. Aldana Frederick Luis, "Unbraiding Tradition: An Interview with Chitra Divakaruni" *Journal of South Asian Literature*. Vol.35. Number 192.2000, p. 6.
15. Banerjee Debjani, *op.cit.*, p.23.
16. Aldana F.L., *op. cit.*, p. 7
17. Selvam Veena, " Mistresses and Sisters Creating a Female Universe: The Novels of Chitra Banerjee Divakaruni" *The Literacy Criterion*. Vol. XXXV –2005. No. 2, p. 54.
18. Sofky Elizabeth, "Cross-cultural Understanding Spiced with the Indian Diaspora". *Black Issues in Higher Education*. Reston: Sep 18,1997. Vol.14, p. 26.
19. Sarah Ann Johnson, "*The Writer*", Boston: March 2004. Vol. 117. P.
20. Chitra Banerjee. *Bold Type*. (1998) 20 Aug. 2000.
21. Chitra Banerjee, *'Do South Asian Women Need Separate Shelter Homes?'* Rediff on the Net (6 July 1999) 20 Aug.2000.
22. Barat Urbashi, "Sister of the Heart: Female Bonding in Fiction of Chitra Banerjee Divakaruni". *Diasporic Imiagination. Asian American Writing*. Vol-2 Fiction: Novels and short stories ed. by Somadatta Manal. Prestige Books. 2000.P.N. -48.
23. *Ibid.*, p. 49.
24. Eswari C.N. "Post-colonialism and Chitra Banerjee's *Sister of My Heart*." *Contemporary Literacy criticism, Theory and Practice*. Vol. II Ed. N.D.R. Chandra. Authors Press, 2003, p. 337.
25. *Ibid.*, p. 339.
26. Johnson Sarah Ann, "*The Writer*" Boston: March 2004 Vol, 117.p. 25.
27. Zaleski Jeff, "The Vine of Desire" *Publishers Weekly*. New York: Nov. 26, 2001, Vol. 248, p. 38.
28. Straddling Two Cultures: Chitra Banerjee Divakaruni. *http://www.calitreview.com/Interviews/intdivakaruni8002.htm*. p. 2.
29. Kinsella Bridget, "Being American in Today's world" *Publishers Weekly*. New York. Aug 9, 2004. Vol. 251, p. 229.

30. *Ibid.*, pp. 229-30
31. *Ibid.*, p. 230.
32. Metroplus the Hindu July 21, 2011 "Trendy Twists to timeless tale" Narshini Vakkalanka.
33. Sarah Ann Johnson, "The Writer" Boston: March 2004, Vol.117. p. 20.
34. *Ibid.*, 21.
35. Email interview with Sanjitha Rao with Chitra Banerjee Weaving Magic Monday 12 May 2008.
36. Bhabha Homi K. *The Location of Culture.* London: Routledge. 1994, p. 1.
37. Banerjee Debjani, *op.cit.*, p. 29.

Chapter 4

The Narrative Art of Bapsi Sidhwa and Chitra Banerjee

The Narrative art of Bapsi Sidhwa and Chitra Banerjee

Narratives are expressions and representations of lived experience even though they may not actually have been lived. Narratives essentially link real life form to art. All narratives have in-built element of universality which make their listeners or readers feel a sense of shared meaning. Narratives of cultural representations inhabit the epistemic construction of the migrant, gendered or ethnic identity. The concept of belonging and unbelonging in relation to that of "space" – real or imaginary have profound impact on the diasporic subject. The narratives of all diasporic writers assert that 'ethnicity' is not something fixed; it evolves and is the result of the lived experience of the migrant. The narrative of the diasporic writer also bring out the truth that the centre margin relationship is basically unstable.

Sukalpa Bhattacharjee comments on the identity crisis and various subjects represented by the narrative of the diasporic writers:

> .....caught in the exchanges between the local and the global, the centre and periphery, the citizenship and the cultural membership, the private and the public, the subjects here are experiencing manifold challenges to locate their self-definition and the narratives of self-identity

characterized by this existential dilemma, the narratives of mixed-blood displaced expatriate and identity here is siege from within in a transition seeking to link late modern cultural and social capital with tradition. A look at the self and the other, therefore, constantly poses a crisis in terms of having a stable definition and hence a stable narrative. [1]

Both Chitra Banerjee and Bapsi Sidhwa live in America and are women of the Indian sub-continent and yet there is an ambience of the locale in their writing. They share a double tradition, which is both Indian and American. Both are good storytellers. They move reader emotionally and the reader can share his or her experience with the character in the fiction. Like most other postcolonial writers- Chitra Banerjee and Bapsi Sidhwa use fictional autobiography as mode of narration, which help them to express the angst, experienced during the process of becoming foreign citizen. Moreover, for an immigrant writer, the act of writing itself becomes a form of purgation. Both writers believe that their own expatriate experience has made them writer. The cultural narratives of Bapsi Sidhwa and Divakaruni portray the world from the margin and the borderlands. These narratives give voice and space to question of the tradition and modernity. Though Sidhwa and Divakaruni have become writers because of their expatriate experiences, their narrative is a fictional exploration of the complexities of belonging and identity, the shifting and cross-cutting cultural experience of diaspora and relocation. Their writing highlights particular post-colonial and minority writings. Their texts are generated out of a particular, but significantly different, migrant or post-colonial condition. Though they are not feminist writers, their narratives are produced by women who face the denial of identity, both within the marginalized community and by the dominant culture. These women are doubly exiled.

Bapsi Sidhwa's narrative skills are rather unsophisticated. Though she rewrites the history and tries to present cruelties of history in almost all her novels but she has a brilliant sense of humour. She explains:

> Laughter does so many things for us. It has the quality of exposing wrongs and gets rid of anger and excitement. [2]

Sidhwa is a notable writer because of her sharp wit and ability to blend humour with social realism. She believes 'humour' brings balance in our life. The overall mode of her novels is comic. In all her novels – *An American Brat, The Crow Eaters, The Pakistani Bride and Ice-Candy Man* Bapsi Sidhwa uses parody, wit, humour, irony and hilarious language to present various themes. *An American Brat* is a humorous portrayal of funny and terrifying perceptions of an upper middle class Parsi family about the life in USA. Bapsi Sidhwa cleverly juxtaposes the first world perception and the third world perception while portraying the expatriate experience. Sidhwa also uses slang to create humour. The politeness of Feroza, is contrasted with the rash Americans in usages of words. Once Feroza went for shopping along with Jo. The following exchange took place between Feroza and the middle aged, wiry little sales woman behind the cosmetics counter. A timid Feroza politely asked:

Can I have a look at some of those hair sprays, Please?"

The glass bangles on her arms jingling, Feroza pointed at an array of hair sprays in a window behind the saleswoman. The nametag pinned to the saleswoman's pink-and-gray striped uniform read "Sally".

"Sure you can, honey. Look all you want, said Sally busy with the cash register. Feroza colored and said, "I mean, can I see some of them up close?

Sally looked her up and down suspiciously as if measuring the degree of "foreignness". She got off the stool behind her register, performing the feat as if descending a mountain, plonked three brands of hair spray on the glass shelf before Feroza, and climbed back to her busy seat.

Feroza read the labels on each and holding the can she had selected timidly forth, nervously adjusting the shawl that had slid off her shoulder ventured, "May I have this please?" You may not. You will have to pay for it. This isn't the Salvation Army y'know, it's a drugstore." (AB-150)

The salesgirl "Sally" thought the foreign girl was asking for charity and replies curtly. Feroza's friend Jo taught her numerous Americanisms so that people don't "stomp all over" her (AB-151).

The polite expressions of 'please' and 'may I' get replaced by 'Gimme a coke' 'Geeme a lemonade', 'Gimme a soda' or "Lemme see' (AB154).

Asians generally speak loudly, especially on telephone, while Americans are soft-spoken. Before coming to America Feroza talked to her uncle Manek on telephone. She shouted, "I'm so exited" Manek is not used to listen to shouting. Manek said, "Don't yell, you are puncturing my eardrum. Why do you Third World Pakis shout so much? Everybody is not deaf".

Sidhwa uses language as a source of humour and contrast of cultures. With the passage of time meanings of certain words get qualified and changed. A dominant group enforces their own usages, pronunciation as correct. The immigrants find difficulty in the beginning to understand the meanings of phrases like "Get off my back", "Give me a break", "Stick it", "I am bushed".(3) A lot of misunderstanding and embarrassment takes place because the immigrants take literal meaning of the phrases. Today world has become a global village. One needs to develop the cross-cultural understanding.

As Divakaruni uses Bengali proverbs, sayings, and words in her novels, Sidhwa uses Gujarathi, Hindi, Urdu proverbs and words in her novels. Their texts have lot of instances of code-mixing:

'Okay baba, Okay, I am going'.

'There was a bit of subdued Khoos-poossing'.

O baapray! Oh dear father!

O Mahra baap! Oh my father! (AB-192-194)

Sidhwa translated Gujrathi idioms into English. Feroza said to her uncle Manek, "Jealous, Is someone's bottom burning?" Manek replied, "Not mine, Must be yours" (AB-224)

One couldn't control laughing while reading such instances. The most successful comedy, one finds is in the novel – *The Crow Eaters.* The protagonist of the main plot, Faredoon Junglewall's mother-in-law, Jerbanoo is a typical character. She was problematic character in Junglewalla's family as she pokes her nose in everyone's personal life. Chapter 42 and 43 depict the visit of Junglewalla's family to London. These chapters show – how crazy, mischeivous this old lady is? She is misfit everywhere. They stayed with Mr. Charles P. Allen. Jerbanno was not satisfied with their breakfast, life-style. Sometime her remarks are India-personal, India-insulting:

> Why you not make curry today? Why you not cut onion proper? Why you not rinse O. K.? I do not drink with soap! 'No chilli? I no digest!' 'Why you not wear nice long gown? silly frock, It shows you got a terrible leg'. Why you not have bath! Water bite you?'. 'You sit, you drink tea-cup every two, two minutes. Mind demon of laziness makes your bottom fat. (CE-255-56)

The height Jerbano made is beyond imagination. She jacked up Mrs. Allen's skirt with a fork from the dining table. Only Sidhwa can write the text with such a dramatic effect. The novel brings out the humour arising out of the verbal clash between Jerbano's pidgin and the English man's dialect. The climax of humour takes place when Junglewalla had to shift in hotel because of the stupidity of Jerbano. Being a good Indian woman, she can't do without daily baths. To avoid common bathroom Jerbano had a wonderful idea of taking bath in the walled balcony. While taking bath, she has no idea of drainage system till she hears from below: "Blimy! God was being flooded!" (CE-266). But she manages the situation with arrogance. She was very adamant.

Makrand Paranjpe compares Bapsi Sidhwa with Chaucer and Shakespeare while discussing various dimensions of comic mode in *The Crow Eaters:*

> *The Crow Eaters* thus explores both the superficial and the more profound dimensions of the comic mode. Not only is it an entertaining satire and farce on the foibles of its main characters, but it also embodies a larger vision of the world, a vision which is best described as broad, tolerant, and sympathetic. This vision is comic in the same sense as Chaucer's vision or Shakespeare's in his comedies are comic, for it tries to convey the variety, diversity, vitality and validity of life at all points. (4)

The Crow Eaters is no doubt autobiographical text but Bapsi Sidhwa turns it into art by her clever use of irony, humour. The novel highlights both the shortcomings and achievements of the Parsi community along with their identity crisis. As the Parsis settled in India, they realized they can survive as a minority in India only by being loyal to every ruling authority. So the sycophancy is shown as a 'need to exist' in the case of Faredoon Jurglewalla in *The Crow Eaters* when he visits to government house to pay homage to the British Empire. Faredoon Junglewalla achieves fame, wealth and status after settling in North Indian cities. But certain doubts are raised because there is paradox in his characters. The novel begins with his character sketch:

> Faredoon Junglewala, Freddy for short, was a striking handsome, dulcet-voiced adventurer with so few sruples that he not only succeeded in carving a comfortable niche in the world for himself but he also earned the respect and gratitude of his entire community. when he died at sixty-five, a majestic grey-haired patriarch, he attained the rare distinction of being locally listed in the Zarathusti calendar of Great Men women. (CE-9)

But the novel clearly shows that his fame and wealth have dubious roots. His life is full of contradictions. Through the narrative of Freddy, Sidhwa balances personal inadequacies against the contradictions of life itself. Therefore in the novel irony is also a mode of acceptance a type of philosophy one has to understand with the passage of time. Freddy gives some lessons of survival to his community:

'And where, if I may ask, does the sun rise?

'No, Not in the East. For us it rises – and sets-in the Englishman's arse. They are our sovereigns! Where do you think we'd be if we did not curry favour? Next to the nawabs, rajas and princelings, we are the greatest toadies of the British Empire! These are not ugly words mind you. They are the sweet dictates of our delicious need to exist, to live and prosper in peace otherwise, where would we Parsis be? Cleaning out gutters with the untouchables – a dispersed pinch of snuff sneezed from the heterogeneous nonstrils of India! Oh yes, in looking after our interests we have maintained our strength – the strength to advance the grand cosmic plan of Ahura Mazda – the deep spiritual law which governs the universe, the path of *Asha*. (CE-12)

Freddy's flattery, exaggerated servility towards British reveals Parsis underlying identity crisis and quest of security in India. But the English refused to consider Parsees as their own kind even if they were equally educated and extensively anglicized. Parsees were also inspired by the prevailing social milieu and they developed dislike to identifying themselves with other Indian communities. Because they know they will not be benefited by partition.

Bapsi Sidhwa uses irony to show ambivalent attitude towards charity. A number of instances of Freddy's charity are shown in the novel:

And once you have the means, there is no end to the good you can do. I donated towards the construction of an orphanage and a hospital. I installed a water pump with a stone plaque dedicating it my friend. Mr. Charles P Allen. (CE-10)

Once Freddy helped his friend's son Boby Kartak escape police charges for killing a beggar whilst rashly driving. Freddy always pose to everyone that he is the saint – always ready to help other. He turned to Mr. Katrak:

'I talked to my friend; you know who I mean. I pleaded with him that the boy is like my own son. He says he will

> try and get him off the hook. I convinced him it was not Bobby's fault, but since he did not report the accident the charges are grave... Anyway, my friend promises to help...but.....the bastard wants fifty thousand rupees!' (CE-153-54)

Freddy gave only ten thousand rupees to Mr. Gibbons the Inspector General of Police and stowed away the remaining forty in his special kitty. Bapsi Sidhwa in ironic tone comments – "This was the kitty he dipped into help others and occasionally himself". (CE-154)

Only Bapsi Sidhwa can use irony, ambivalent attitude to create such a humour. Irony in this novel highlights the Parsee paradox. Novy Kapadia comments on the comic mode of *The Crow Eaters* and the broad vision of life that Bapsi Sidhwa has:

> The overall mode of the novel is comic. It is not a social comedy like that of Jane Austen or a satirical comedy of Swift or a comedy of manners – but is a genial comedy. The view of life of Bapsi Sidhwa is expansive. Human foibles and follies are treated with tolerance and mild corrective irony. (5)

The purpose of Bapsi Sidhwa is not teaching or accepting or disapproving the paradox of the Parsee community but to present their marginal personality and hybridity, which they acquire with the movements of time.

Bapsi Sidhwa interweaves satirical fiction, wit and humour to depict historical facts, which she has, witness as a child. In her third novel – *Cracking India,* Lenny, 8 years old girl is a narrator. Like Sidhwa, Lenny is stricken with polio, lives in Lahore, and is a Parsi. Like Sidhwa she is shrewd observant narrator. After reading the novel, reader feels Lenny's character is too intelligent for her age. Narendrakumar has rightly observed about the two narratives, which Sidhwa has employed in the novel:

> The first is that of Lennie, a child and other is that of authorial omniscient narrative voice. Lennie's rendering is through her dreams and nightmares. It is more

> subjective, though not involved or enlightened about its consequences. The other is an implied adult narration trying to objectify what is child's narration, however precocious she may be. (6)

Being a Parsee and employing a child narrator, Sidhwa provides impartial, disinterested, near factual description of partition in *Cracking India.* The Ice-Candy Man symbolizes evil/leaders responsible for partition and the absolute suffering of ordinary people on either side of the border. Ayah, who look after Lenny symbolizes Mother Earth. Though Sidhwa is not aware of allegorical references while writing the novel – *Cracking India,* allegory becomes one of the important structural principles, which controls the narrative. According Sidhwa, Ayah Symbolises – India:

> Ayah, for instance, is not symbolic of anything, but on reflection, I felt that she could be representing India in a way. These are people who desire her so much, and each one of them, when he has a chance, ravishes her. [7]

The ultimate analysis of *Cracking India* provides Ayah and Ice-Candy Man as personifications of ideas- the former stands of Mother India/Earth and the latter for Evil/Politicians responsible for bloodshed, dislocation after partition. The growth of child narrator is shown against the backdrop of partition. For all Indian novelists (who are sufferer of the partition) and Sidhwa, partition is not a mere historical event but an all-inescapable emotional experience.

Cracking India is a parallel story of the history of Lenny and the chronological development of partition tale. Sidhwa, like other postcolonial writers, rewrites the history in 'English' from the Parsee perspective. Each post-colonial novelist creates his own 'space' of authenticity and belongingness by his 'English'. Thus Sidhwa, offers reinterpretation of history from women's perspective. Being a supporter for women's right in the increasingly fundamentalist milieu of Pakistan, Sidhwa produces a certain variety of post-colonial nationalist feminism as a project for *Cracking India*. Through this novel Sidhwa tries to show women's victimization by male rivalries.

Thousands of women were kidnapped. Terrible venedettas were enacted on their bodies to humiliate the men of another faith. According to Ambreen Hai the novel *Cracking India* portrays:

> .....in its very form of personal, autobiographical narration, the novel strives to substitute one dominant kind of historiography (masculinist, totalizing, exclusivist, (neo) colonial, impersonal, national) with an alternate one (partial, multiple, non-teleological, grounded in collective experience) (8)

The novel also questions the place of women within a heavily gendered nationalism. Through the narrative of Godmother and Lenny's mother, Sidhwa highlights the restorative work done by Parsee community particularly border women who constructs a refuge for "fallen women" of all religion. Ambreen Hai has rightly pointed the focus of Sidhwa's narrative:

> As a Parsee Pakistani woman's writing contingent upon belonging / unbelonging, it attempts to build a usefully skewed national identity and suggests new modes of creating trans-ethnic and trans-religious alliances. It thus upholds the power of border feminism (as emblematized by Parsee women) to redress the causalities of neo-colonial history. (9)

Thus Sidhwa's narrative celebrates both border crossing and border inhabitation, In *Cracking India,* Sidhwa portrays life and time in the subcontinent during the British Raj between the period 1935 to 1947. The narrative of the novel constructs history in all its consequences in the dramatic portrayal of interaction among various communities, their habits, belief, religions politics and ethos. The episodic structure of novel describes through Lenny's eye, the pain, stupidity suffering, joy before and after the partition of India in Lahore.

Tripathi Vaneshree has compared Bapsi Sidhwa's narration of history with Rushdie, Tharoor and Khushwant Singh. Tripathi Vaneshree writes:

> *Ice-Candy Man* is a sincere and successful effort to artistically portray the life in the subcontinent at a crucial juncture history without indulging in hostile parodistic melodrama or extravagant, vociferous pyrotechniques one may find in the recent subcontinent fiction. While the latest novels by Rushdie, Tharoor or Khushwant Singh appears to be guided by a self-conscious, subversive ideology, Sidhwa's "truth telling" narration transcribes the destructive impulse of time with such compassion in an unpretentious idiom that even most anaesthetized or cynical reader feels touched. Feeling flows in the narrative not intended to shock or to impress but to make us identify the marginalized culture outside the mainstream as a part of history. (10)

Sidhwa's novel- *Cracking India/ Ice Candy Man* moves readers emotionally – may be because it is female's perspective of history and her comprehensive out look of life.

South Asian American writers – especially women and ethnic writers in America and elsewhere, rewrite the novel of education or formation through their feminist project. Sidhwa, Bharti Mukherjee, Meena Alexander and Chitra Banerjee Divakaruni re-interprets the issue such as – gender relations, nationalism and identity construction in their homeland and chosen land. Maria Karafilis one of the feminist scholars observes:

> Many writers of color, both ethnic American and post-colonial, use the Bildungsroman to affirm and assert the complex subjectivities of their characters and by extension, themselves. (11)

This women writer challenges the limiting narratives including humanism, misogyny and orientalism. Till now the writing of these writers was invisible. But now it has become visible as they reshape the cannon of American literature. These writers make feminist interventions into narrative and cultural traditions. Their novels are political documents, which reveal important trends of the contemporary South Asian experience in America and their subcontinent. Their novels also depict the transnational literary and cultural development in the world. Through their character, especially female protagonist they try to understand themselves as an individual within multicultural America. They combine their personal narratives of development, which are in 'flux' with national and international analysis.

Their expatriate experience constitutes the core of the narrative in the novel. When one compares Bapsi Sidhwa and Chitra Banerjee with Bharti Mukherjee, it becomes clear that – Sidhwa's and Banerjee's roots continue to exist in their subcontinent. On the contrary Bharti Mukherjee rejects her Indian Identity to become "truly" American. Though experience of exile plays an important role in Bapsi Sidhwa's writing, she never feels exiled because she goes back to Pakistan again and again. Bapsi Sidhwa and Bharati Mukherjee differ radically from each other, although both are expatriate novelists. Bapsi Sidhwa's canvas is broader than Mukherjee's. Along with expatriate experience, she writes about relevant issues such as mixed marriage, oppression of women, and status of Parsee community after partition. In *An American Brat* Sidhwa writes about the growing Islamic fundamentalism in Pakistan and its impact on the ethnicity of Parsee community – particularly women.

Dimple Basu in *Wife* (written by Bharati Mukherjee) and Feroza Ginwalla in *An American Brat* move to America. The difference between Dimple and Feroza is that – Dimple moved to America after marriage and Feroza before marriage. In *Wife* the narrative focuses on the complexities of diaspora in the sensitive mind of Dimple. She has developed various fantasies with her life. She always compares her life with exhilarating women on TV. She is totally dissatisfied with her life, she never believes in family values. As she is secretly prone to violent fantasies which reject the possibility of meaningful relationships with either her husband Amit and various Indian women she meets in America or her temporary lover Milt. She finds her life constricted and dull first at her in-laws house in India and then alone in America with Amit.

The end of the narrative shows Dimple's inability to take pleasure in her own life leads her to murderous act and abortion.

Both Feroza and Dimple are typical migrants. But Feroza's alienation in *An American Brat* is positive and Dimple's alienation is tragically negative. Feroza shows increasing levels of adaptability in America. On the contrary, Dimple's adaptability level is zero. Feroza preserves her ethnic identity and her ethnicity helps her for successful assimilation into American life. Dimple remains a "Permanent alien". Though Feroza experiences cultural shocks, including threads to her physical safety, verbal humiliation and racist treatment, she is a luckier immigrant. Being a young and unmarried, the dream of America holds more shiny promise to her because she has chance for living independent life. But Feroza's emotional involvement with David Press, an American Jew comes as a potent threat to the orthodox Parsee community of Lahore. Zareen her mother came to America to dissuade Feroza from marrying David but ironically she modifies her stand on mixed marriage. She begins to question the rigid codes of Parsee community, which are responsible for extinction of Parsee community:

> How could a religion whose prophet urged his followers to spread the truth of his message in the holy Gathas – the songs of Zarathustra – prohibit and throw her daughter out of faith? (AB-287)

She would like to support Parsee teenagers on their stand on mixed marriages; she believes there should be some reforms taken by the Zoroastrian Anjumans in Karachi and Bombay. Bapsi Sidhwa skillfully employs a situation in the narrative which suggests the demand of rethinking in the Parsee community. Through the narrative of Zareen and Feroza, she hints at the need of change. She emphasizes on the need for a compromise on crucial issues like mixed marriages as the survival of the microscopic community is at risk. The narrative of Feroza ends in her positive assimilation in America. Thus Feroza discovers the "privacy" and "flexibility" in America and decided to live permanently in America. This new world offers Feroza adequate social space to grow and Zoroastrianism provides the ultimate emotional and religious space to her.

The salient features of post-colonial fiction are the use of several intertexual references and also writing some idioms, words which reflect the author's cultural background. *Ice-Candy Man/ Cracking India* begins with lines of Iqbal:

> Shall I hear the lament of the nightingale, submissively lending my ear? Am I the rose to suffer its cry in silence year after years?

The fire of verse gives me courage and bids me no more to be faint. With dust in my mouth I am object: to God I make my complaint. Sometimes you favour our rivals then sometimes with us you are free. I am sorry to say it so boldly; you are no less fickle than we. (Iqubal Complaint to God) (CI-1)

These lines by Iqubal serve as a prologue to novel. These lines depict the wrenching pain of partition which people has undergone and still people are paying price for it. Sidhwa catch Ice Candy Man's anguish of separation in the words of another romantic poet, Ghalib:

> My passion has brought me to year street – where can I now find the strength to take me back? (CI-277)

To show the maturity of Ice-Candy Man and how he has become a truly harmless fellow, Sidhwa quotes the lines of Zauq:

> 'Why did you make a home inhabit it. Both the house and I am desolate. Am I a thief that your watchman stops me? Tell him, I know this man. He is my fate' (CI-276)

> 'Don't berate me, beloved, I am God-intoxicated! I will wrap myself about you; I am mystically mad' (CI-277)

All these lines reflect the wisdom of Ice Candy Man. He understands the truth of life. These lines also show Sidhwa's fascination for Urdu Poets – Iqbal and Ghalib. These intertexual references enable Sidhwa not only to register 'cultural distance' but also to introduce the exotic to the western reader.

Various newspapers, authors has written a words of praise for Bapsi Sidhwa's *Ice-Candy Man/ Cracking India* as Sidhwa captures the turmoil of times with development of Leny. Following are the words of praise from the Literary Review which highlight the theme and narrative technique of *Ice-Candy Man*:

> Sidhwa's Rabelaisian language and humour are enormously refreshing especially in context of modern Indian fiction, which has tended rather towards the prim and stilted. In *Ice-Candy Man*, as in her previous novels, she succeeds in transmitting into English much of the spirit of Punjabi language and culture, which is nothing if not earthy. But her prose is also both delicate and precise in its imagery and descriptions, with words chosen as carefully as pieces of inlay in a marble wall. (The Literary Review) (CI).

In almost all her novels she uses multiple plots to reflect to the complexities of life. Though many parallel stories are there in novels, they are unified because of theme. For example in the novel *The Bride* – the story of Zaitoon and Carol highlights one of the key issues in the novel - the position and treatment of women in society. Markarand R Paranjape has rightly observed Bapsi Sidhwa's narrative art, which is very simple, but even then it can heighten the emotions of reader:

> Sidhwa's is a plain, matter of fact, supple style, without ornate flourishes or unnecessary complications, yet it can rise to poetic intensity when the narrative demands it. Hers is a consistent unselfconscious "middle style" (12)

Sidhwa has full control over her language. Diversity is striking feature of her writing as it deals with various ranges of settings, plots, themes and characters.

Both Bapsi Sidhwa and Chitra Banerjee come close to the recent experimental writer in the post-colonial fiction like

Salman Rushdie, who deal with history from the perspective of present. They rewrite history from their perspectives. Their narrative celebrates the will; resolve to resist evil, and the struggle against oppression of women. Their writings are the stories of courage and heroism, which has great dramatic intensity.

According to Sukalpa Bhattacharjee :

> Chitra Banerjee's other novels like *The Mistress of Spices, Arranged Marriage* and particularly *The Unknown Errors of Lives* are sensuously filled with images. Her novels have been described intensely touching tales of lapsed communication, inarticulate love and redemptive memories. (13)

Chitra Banerjee's texts as a narrative try to bridge not only distinct national identities but also find a place within for the dislocated gender. The stories narrated in her text have two threads – one of dominant culture and other ethnic sub culture. As one undergoes emotional, cultural and geographical displacement, these two threads may intermingle and it becomes difficult to identify 'ours' and 'theirs'. The outcome of displacement and resettlement is "hybrid" identity, which can also be called as "liminal" Salman Rushdie, has rightly pointed:

> Our identity is at once plural and partial. We straddle two cultures (14)

An immigrant loses something in the transition and at the same time he gains something. These pluses and minuses are depicted by the narrative of the text of Chitra Banerjee. In present day world, globalized practices of metropolis have radically changed the demographics and subjectivities of Asian raced people in the United States. Lowe, Lisa feels the need of retheorization of issues related to Asian American people:

> "Oppression", "marginalization", and "resistance", keywords in dominant narratives of Asian American studies, are terms that each require redefinition within this globalized context, as 'by whom" and "against what"

are questions that are increasingly difficult to answer with certitude. (15)

Chitra Banerjee depicts the struggle of middle-class Asian American women- some of them are housewives and some are workingwomen. Sau- ling C. Wong writes about the place of the middle-class Asian American women in the United State:

> Nevertheless, by the 1990s, granting extreme heterogeneity within the Asian American population and continued dominance of white men in the wage scale, certain segments of middleclass Asian American women have done well enough for impressions of superlative success to emerge. Often middle-class Asian American women are simultaneously positioned to be the powerful in some situations (for example, when they perform managerial roles) and the marginalised in other (for example, when the same women suffer workplace racial discrimination) A range of interpellative possibilities, have opened up for middle-class Asian American women in master narratives of immigrant success (for the foreign-born), ethnic assimilation, feminist liberation, capitalist consumerism, liberal multiculturalism, global mobility, and others. (16)

The presence of multiple and changing subjectivities has enabled ethnic women writers of Africa and Indian Sub-Continent to shed their invisibility and articulate a voice and occupy a visible space in the American society. Ethnic women writers like Toni Morrison, Gloria Naylor, Maya Angleoue, Jhumpa Lahiri, Bapsi Sidhwa and Chitra Banarjee Divakaruni are using the text to wrest their own meaning from the patriarchal cultural practices and create their own "space" in the United State. Their narrative helps to reconstruct the cultural institution.

Chitra Banerjee uses different story telling techniques- the first person narrative, the third person narrative, interior monologue, epistolary exchange, diary entries and stream of consciousness dream sequences. These various techniques help her to convey the pain and confusion of Indian immigrants during the process of assimilation. Divakaruni uses the first person narrative form in her novel *Sister of My Heart*. She uses alternative mode of narration – Anju and Sudha narrate their stories alternatively in the first person. This first person narration endows them to tell their stories powerfully and help them to shape their reality. Their aunt Pishi use to tell them various stories. Once she told them about the popular belief in their community – that the night after a child is born, the deity Bidhata Purushu comes down to earth to decide its destiny. The disappearance of the sweetmeats kept near the child during the night is indicative of his blessing. Aunt Pishi told them that in their case the sweetmeats never disappear. Their aunt wants to suggest that women are doomed to suffer. Instead of surrendering to such suggestion, the narrative 'I' incase of Anju, gives her power to break the tradition and have her own control over her life. But Sudha is more traditionally oriented. C. N. Eswari has rightly pointed the use of the first person narrative by Divakaruni in the *Sister of My Heart* :

> In *Sister of My Heart,* Anju's first person narration is used to reflect the mounting conflict between the two cultures and its ultimate resolution in the writer's mind. The narrative 'I' lends a personal perspective to the situation and helps in bridging the gap between the diverse culture, and the separate vision of reality. A cross-cultural identity is established not by reconciling one culture to another or by subordinating one to another but by giving equal validity to both. An authorial intimacy pervades the novel through the deft handling of the pseudo autobiographical form. (17)

Though *Sister of My Heart* is full of conventional myth and mysteries, Divakaruni rejects conventional myths and creates new one. The mythic framework of *Sister of My Heart* and *Mistress of Spices* contributes to the creation of a female universe. In both the novel there is an attempt to create fresh myths or at least give new interpretations to existing ones. The first book in the novel *Sister of My Heart* is titled *The*

Princess in the Palace of snakes. In this part both the protagonists – Anju and Sudha follow the traditional feminine roles allocated by the male hegemonic society. This is symbolized by the traditional fairytale of the princess in the palace of Snakes waiting for her Prince charming to rescue her. The second book of the novel is titled *The Queen of Swords.* This is not traditional fairytale. When Anju is upset over her miss-carriage Sudha tells her this tale and Anju recovers. Here Divakaruni remytholises the fairytale told by Sudha:

> Once there was a princess who spent her girlhood in a crumbling marble places set around with guards. They told her what was proper and what was not, and held up their poison spears before her face if she attempted to stray outside the boundaries they had drawn for her ....The Queen held her daughter with one hand and with the other she grasped the rainbow. And her sister pulled her across the ocean, over the gaping jaws of sea monster to safety. (SH 308-310)

Divakaruni remytholises the fairytale by showing how the protagonist found safety beyond male world. Here rescuer is female not male. The princess in the story is mythic representation of Sudha who instead of accepting Ashok's help, go to America. Sudha's journey to America is really the beginning of her journey to a new world of women. Their mothers also enter this new world of women. This is symbolically shown when they sell their ancestral home and shift to a new flat. They started living fulfilling life – they listen to the music that they like and take walks where they please. They are free from the pressures of society.

Chitra Banerjee has shown through her novels – *Sister of My Heart* and *Vine of Desire* that nothing can separate Sudha and Anju. Perhaps because of this, she tells her novels are of women's friendship, not of sisterly bond. The short stories "Affair" and "Meeting Mrinal" are about the quest of selfhood and friendship; But Divakaruni considers friendship as her main theme. Urbhashi Bharat writes about the place of 'women's friendship' in the Western fiction:

> Women friendships in Western fiction have undoubtedly suffered when women have weighed them against feminine duties and responsibilities towards parents, lovers and husbands and children. Thus, in Jane Eyre the protagonist must outgrow her friendship with Helen Burns before she can enter the world of adulthood; and Helen must die, and Mr. Rochester's other women, Bertha Mason, Celine Varens and Blanche be silenced, Marginalized, and defeated in order that Jane triumphantly take her position as his wife and mother of his children. (18)

Toni Morrison believes that her novel *Sula* is the first novel dealing with female friendship. The protagonist Sula Peace and Nel Wright grow up together in a small back neighborhood in Medallion, Ohio. They were close friends because they have many things in common and they are different in many ways. Sula and Nel are similar to Anju and Sudha in *Sister of My Heart.* Like Sudha, Nel marries and settles down to a conventional family. Like Anju, Sula has quest of selfhood. Sula begins her experiments with life, which includes sexual encounter with Nel's husband. Nel cannot accept this betrayal on Sula's part. Sula is shocked as they have always shared the affection of other people. After the death of Sula, Nel realizes that without Sula her life is incomplete. Morrison suggests that women's friendship is deeper, more permanent than any other relationship.

Like Meena and Abha in the story "Affair" from *Arranged Marriage,* Nel and Sula have always shared their lives together. Abha is miserable and jealous with Meena but her focus of jealousy is different; Meena had not told her about the affair herself:

> *How could you have done this to me, Meena?* At first I wasn't sure if I meant the affair itself or the fact that it was with Ashok, or that she had kept it from me. Then I knew I could have forgiven her the first one, and even the second, if only she hadn't done the third. (AM 266)

When Abha meets Meena to sort out matters with her, she discovers her friend is having an affair with Charles and not with her husband Ashok. Divakaruni's women face different situation. They love their men and they think their men also love them. They suffered when they realized, they are betrayed by their friends. But they quickly realize that their friend is different from their love for their husband. Friendship to all Divakaruni's protagonists is more important than their men. Friendship therefore surpasses all other relationship – especially hetro-sexual. Nel and Sula had learned this too late which Sudha and Anju (*Sister of My Heart*), Abha and Meena ("Affair") learned in good times.

In *The Vine of Desire,* Divakaruni has use various narrative techniques such as letters, omniscient narrative, the telling of folk tales and stories, film narratives, internal monologues and scholarly papers. Divakaruni uses these various techniques to break down the boundary between the realistic, contemporary inner-city world and the world of magic to show that they do coexist. Divakaruni gives the reason behind using these various techniques together in *The Vine of Desire:*

> In *The Vine of Desire,* I was working on breaking down different forms and genres ....I was trying to break down the differences between these forms and create a unity in terms of a central thematic experience of desire, which all the characters are going through and learning to deal with (19)

In *The vine of Desire,* Divakaruni use letters to convey information about Sudha and Anju's lives. Divakaruni explained the reason for using letter format:

> The letter format is very interesting because in letter, the characters become the writer and can therefore shape the reality they want to convey. The letters are not just telling what has happened; they're also revealing certain things and hiding other things. There are the aborted letters that are never sent. You see them in the text of Vine with lines through them. I was able to play with ideas of, what is really happening? How far do the characters understand

it? How does the character select which details to give to other characters and which to withhold. The letters become an ironic device as well as a powerful emotional tool. Sometimes you can write about things that you can't tell someone face to face. Letters can be more of a confession than you would otherwise make. (20)

These letters writing from Anju to Sudha, Sudha to Anju, Anju to her mother, Pishi Aunt to Sudha, and Sunil to Anju make the novel *The Vine of Desire* more realistic. The skillful use of these various techniques and styles allow the reader a unique access in to the complex consciousness of each of the characters- including men. One discovers here that Sunil is a lonely man suffering from an absent father. He is afraid of taking risks so he has to live an incomplete life. Sunil writes a letter to Anju before leaving for India.

Houston

September 1994.

Anju-

I respect your wish to be left alone. I won't trouble you with any further communication. However, you are always welcome to write to me. I'm leaving for India to help my mother put her finances in order. In don't know when I'll return. I'm going to give up apartment in California- I guess there is no reason in keeping it, now that you seem to have found a place that suits you better. I hope you'll let me have an address, in case of emergency.

I ask you for one last favor. Can you pack my things? I've called the manager. She'll put them in storage, but I just didn't want her snooping through them. Of course I am in no position to insist, I know that,

I'm enclosing the package for Dayita. Should you know where she is, I would be much obliged if you would forward it to her.

Sunil

P. S. You're still furious with me because I want to end my marriage. But be honest with yourself. Were you happy with the way we were, even when we were together? In our hearts, hadn't we already left each other a long time back? (VD-272-73)

These letters help us to read the mind of the character to some extent. Otherwise one might have misunderstood Sunil.

Divakaruni begins the novel *The Vine of Desire* with physical details:

> In the beginning was pain or perhaps it was the end that was suffused with pain, its distinctive indigo tint color of old bruises, color of broken pottery, of crumpled maps in evening light. But, no, not like them ultimately. For although men have tired for thousand of years to find the right simile-and women, too- ultimately pain is only like itself. (VD P.3)

In this novel Divakuruni textures the experiences of Calcutta born and raised sisters Anju and Sudha, living as adult women in 1990s San Francisco, as they journey through the many colors of pain that are necessary for their discovery of self-worth in an oppressive society. Divakaruni uses physical details to show that we can only feel pain and we cannot express. Divakaruni explains to Sarah Johnson, the way she has used physical detail to help the reader enter the emotional landscape of a narrative:

> It is hard to talk about it, because such thing comes from an intuitive place in me. That line goes on to stay that none of this is True because ultimately, pain is only like it self. I was exploring the idea of how far can you describe emotion and at some point, paradoxically, emotion can only be felt by the person who is feeling it. We can only approximate what that person is feeling. That becomes one of the major themes of *The Vine of Desire*. All these characters, which are entangle with each other, they understand each other only up to a point. [21]

Divakaruni uses images to create the mood that helps reader to understand an emotion, which the character is undergoing. In *The Vine of Desire* also characters tell fairy tales throughout the novel. These fairy tales are analogous to the experiences of modern life. For Divakaruni fairy tales are more important. She says:

> Sometimes what happens with my character is when they're trying to figure out what's going on in their lives, they go to these stories as the ways to understand themselves. They see themselves reflected in the stories, or they see someone else whom they do not understand, or they can't deal with in real life, reflected in the stories. Through that reflective medium, they begin to understand and begin to find sympathy for this character. (22)

Commenting on the narrative art of Chitra Banerjee, Jeff Zalski says:

> Divakaruni combines a gift for absorbing narrative with the artistry of a painter. Her lyrical descriptions of the characters inner and outer worlds bring a rich emotional chiaroscuro to an uplifting story about two women who learn to make peace with the difficult choices circumstances have forced upon them. (23)

Apart from Rushdie there are quite few contemporary writers who use the technique of Magic Realism. The experiment of this technique succeeds when novelist use it to express real life. Currently this technique has become fashionable device which amuses, but does not enlighten. Chitra Banerjee successfully employed Magic Realism in her first novel *The Mistress of Spices* (1997). The heroine Tilo is the "Mistress of Spices". Tilo born in India is shipwrecked on a remote island inhabited by women. First Mother imparts her about the power of spices and sends her to California. She can practice her magical power to heal the immigrants, only if she is away from her mortal desires. In this novel Divakaruni injects magic and mysticism into a contemporary urban setting. With the help of supernatural power, magic- Tilo can help customers (who are immigrants) to surmount their sorrows and fulfill their hopes. Daivakaruni's poetic descriptions of various spices are a fascinating mixture of superstition and homeopathic medicine. She writes:

> Yes they (spices) all hold magic, even the everyday American spices you toss unthinking into your cooking pot. You doubt? Ah. You have forgotten the old secrets your mother's mother knew. Here is one of them again: Vanilla beans soaked soft in goat's milk and rubbed on the wrist bone can guard against the evil eye. And here another: A measure of pepper at the foot of the bed, shaped into a crescent, cures you of nightmare.

But the spices of true power are from my birthland, land of ardent poetry, aquamarine feathers. Sunset skies brilliant as blood. (MS. P.3)

According Divakaruni each spice has a day special to it. For turmeric it is Sunday, "When light drips fat and butter-colored into the bins to be soaked up glowing, when you pray to the nine planets for love and luck" (MS.P.13).

Divakaruni personified the spices. The spices speak to Tilo:

> *I am turmeric who rose out the ocean of milk when the devas and Asuras churned for the treasure of the universe. I am turmeric who came after the poison and before the nectar and thus lie in between.(MS.14)*

Steinberg, Sybil S. Comments on Divakaruni's narration:

> Divakaruni writes lush prose with which she infuses the mundane with magic. Like Bharati Mukharjee, She perceptively depicts a cross-section of the Indian immigrant community trapped between traditional values and the American dream. (24)

The Mistress of Spices Adopts a more mature structural configuration in order to discuss the diaspora. Each chapter contains a short description about an individual and their cultural encounter. Novel doesn't have one plot. The text owes much to non written cultural forms like story telling. Reader is involved in the lives of Jaggi, Ahuja's wife, and Geeta. The structure of the novel is totally informal. The oral narratives of the novel allow reader to interact with the various characters in the novel and the storytellers – Tilo. Debjani Banerjee highlights on the form of *The Mistress of spices:*

> The form of the fable is effectively used in the novel. The "fabulous" world of the mistress imparts a surreal quality to the novel; the order of the Mistresses is and is not patriarchy: the structures overlap and specific histories coincide. One advantage of this literary model is that it continually confounds the category of realism; therefore the events in the novel cannot be processed as information. This is significant in a situation where writers from South Asia and the Third World in general are mined for "evidence" of oppression, which can then be provided as "proof" of the regressive nature of these societies. Written for a largely cosmopolitan audience, Mistress does not provide accessible histories that can provide grist to the mill of First World racism. (25)

The use of the Magic Realism technique gave Divakaruni the widest possible scope to exercise her imagination. Many authors lose their hold on structural values of fiction while using this technique but Divakaruni never loses her control over structure.

Divakaruni's short stories adopt different styles of narration compared to *The Mistress spices.* The short stories and the novel *Sister of My Heart* are grounded in a realistic mode of narration. The realistic mode of narration is an appropriate and effective style to present women's search for identify in the South Asian Diaspora. For Divakaruni, crossing literary borders is important. She explains:

> In *Mistress of Spices,* I was working with breaking down different kind of boundaries, first of all, the boundary between poetry and prose. In my language and in my literary tradition, there are not such clear-cut boundaries between these. In the epics, you go back and forth. They are novelistic, yet they are in poetry. If you come to more modern works, they often mix poetry and prose. You'll have stories with sections in poetry. (26)

Thus, she does various experiments in *The Mistress Spices* successfully.

Divakaruni is gifted writer. She uses 'imagery' skillfully and with ease. Her description of the snake (a spirit guide) in the beginning of the novel *Queen of Dreams* (2004) is wonderful:

> Last night snake came to me. I was surprised, though little surprises me nowadays. He was beautiful than I remembered. His plated green shone like rainwater on banana plants in the garden plot we used to tend behind the dream caves. But may be as I grow older I begin to see beauty where I never expected it before (QD P.1)

In chapter 39 she describes the restlessness of Rakhi in the *Queen of Dreams*:

> All night I can't sleep. My brain feels hot and perforated; my eyes itch as though I'm coming down with an illness. Thoughts thud through my head like a herd of elephants. (QD – 315)

In all most all her fiction, short stories, Divakaruni depicts the Bengali culture, tradition, 'sayings', which help protagonists to face their life. All protagonists experience the 'sayings' told by their mother on different occasion in their life:

> *Using a hair dryer kills your brain cells. Don't go to bed holding on to a grudge.* (QD P. 315)
>
> *The love of good man can save your life.* (UE – 89)
>
> *The stars are the eyes of the dead.* (UE – 92)
>
> *Out of bluest, lightning strikes.* (UE – 93)
>
> *Anger is great destroyer* (UE – 96)

These 'sayings' give inner strength to the character, which help in evolving a new 'identity' in their own land and an adopted land.

There are a lot of instances of intertexuality in her writing. She refers to Shakespeare, Virginia Woolf and many other writers:

> My scientist husband looks at me, bewildered
>
> "Shakespeare", I say. "*As you Like It*" put it on your reading list". (UE – 96)

In *Sister of My Heart*, she writes about many authors. Anju, the protagonist says:

> When I got older, I persuaded mother to order all Woolf's novels, and whenever she allowed me to accompany her to the store, I would go into a corner and devour them. I was afraid someone would want to buy one before I finished it. But they were never popular with our Indian literati, who much preferred Dickens and Hardy and E. M. Forster (SH – 135)

The novel, *A Room of One's Own* by Woolf has moved Divakaruni completely. Anju's husband, Sunil could win her heart only by the books of Virginia Woolf. Anju loves literature. More than her marriage she is happy because after her marriage she will go to America and continue her college. She imagines:

> I clasp his hand as firmly as I can, otherwise I will surely float 'away', my heart is so light. Now that he has discarded his glasses, I see his eyes little flecks of gold in them. Already I adore her crooked eyebrows. I look forward to the evenings when we'll read *To The Lighthouse* together. (S H 137)

In *The Vine of Desire*, Divakaruni writes about the creative journey of Anju. Anju's teacher has given her various assignments.

'Assignment'

Write an essay examining the effects of culture and heredity upon an individual. Would you say they are more important than character traits in influencing the individual's behaviours? You may support your analysis with personal as well as historical/social examples (Approximately fifteen hundreds) (VD – 98)

What is peculiar about Divakaruni is, she gives minute details of the character's life – their childhood, their dreams, their emotional journey, mental traumas and creative journey which ultimately give outlet to them. In chapter eight and fourteen assignments are given to Anju. Anju complete the assignments and remarks of teacher are also included in these chapter. The titles of the assignments written by Anju's are as follow:

Loss: An Essay
By
Anju Majumdar
For
English 3353
Advanced composition
Prof. P. Gossen *(VD – 98)*

My name is Sunil
By
Anju Majumdar
For English 3162
Memoir
Prof. W. Lindley *(CD – 163)*

The first person narrative, letters, these assignments, and scholarly papers provide sufficient 'space' for character to grow and reader gets a clear picture of the character's life. The assessment done by Anju's teacher is very significant for the development of narrative art in Anju's writing. Her teacher remarks:

Ms. Majumdar

Interesting subject matter, though it responds to the assignment in a rather tangential way. Can you give more specific examples in the beginning to help us visualize your mother's life and times?

Your prose style is strong but the paragraph structure is some what unorthodox ...

I notice a number of fragments in the draft. I am not convinced they are necessary. You mention a number of characters without explaining who they are. This is confusing. Try to move your draft from writer-based prose to reader-based prose...

Please, revise accordingly and turn it in by May 15. P. Gossen

P.S. I am disturbed by the events you refer to at the end of the paper. I suggest you pay a visit to counseling (312 Herne Hall) (VD - 102)

Lot of improvement is there in Anju's writing. But the teacher asks her to control emotions while writing essay:

> Ms. Majumdar,
>
> This is well written and powerful in its impact, but a bit of a surprise. It's more of a dramatic monologue (which we do not cover in this class) than a character sketch, which is what I'd asked for.
>
> The character of Sunil is a strong one, though somewhat monodimentional. I am not sure this assignment has helped you understood him further. The narrative intelligence in the essay is not sufficiently male (too emotional) Can you work on this? ...
>
> I am not sure how you will work this into a full-length memoir piece. Maybe you should just start over with a subject you feel less emotional about.
>
> *William Lindley* (VD – 16)

As a child Divakaruni has read a lot of Indian fairy tales, folk tales. She has heard a lot tales from her grandfather and her mother. Therefore a lot of mythical ideas are woven from Indian culture in her writing. In *The Conch Bearer*, the conch is an object of power. Through the world of magic Divakaruni portrays the real world. The novel helps children to cope up with multicultural world. Publisher's Weekly highlights on the Divakaruni's art of story telling:

> Divakaruni keeps her tale fresh and riveting with details of India's sights, smells, and tastes, with characters that possess both good and evil, and with her exploration of the fine line between faith and magic. Young readers can only hope for more from this master story teller." (27)

So many fantasies are being published such as series of *Harry Potter*. But the special about *The Conch Bearer* is its unique setting. The minute details in the story of the slums of 'Calcutta' offer readers a colourfull snapshot of India and its culture. The traditional story is retold in fresh new clothing, which appeals to readers of contemporary world.

The novel-*Queen of Dreams* has a strong narrative, dreams journal entries. Divakaruni combines the Indian American experience with magic realism. The novel effectively portrays that the search for identity and a sense of emotional completion, is not confined to the small corners of the world. It is a dilemma that all readers can feel. After Rakhi's mother's death, Rakhi started reading the dream-journal of her mother. She wanted to know more about India and her connection to Indian culture but her life was shaken by new horrors. After 9/11 she has to deal with complexities about her acculturation. Her mother was a dream teller. Her mother can interpret the dream of others; she can foresee and guide them. But Rakhee's mother hides her knowledge from her. After her death Rakhi started reading the dream journal. In chapter 11, the meanings of various dreams were given:

> Notes, Lesson 17: The meaning of Things.
>
> If you dream of a closed door, you will ultimately be successful in gaining what you desire, but it will take much effort. A dream of milk means you are about to fall ill.

A mirror stands for a false friend, a pair of scissors for a break in a marriage; ..... an iron wheel for ill fortune coming at you from every direction ....

Listen then to the significance of trees: A tree with glossy green leave means a patient's health will improve; a tree that is cut down in a dream means a big expense is about to fall upon you. A palm tree presages good luck, especially if you are climbing it .... A banana tree will bring you an inheritance. A date tree warns you that you must undertake a pilgrimage. (QD 85-86)

Rakhi found her mother's dream journal, full of mystry, superstition. The American born Rakhi couldn't understand this world of supernatural and suspense. San Francisco Chronicle has rightly pointed about the narrative style and theme of the *Queen of Dreams*:

Magical, in lyrical, poetic prose, Divakaruni manages to be hopeful without offering false reassurances, showing how identity both individual and communal is equally shaped by loss and creation. (28)

Divakaruni's latest novel The Palace of Illusions is based on Indian epic Mahabharata. Draupadi is the central character of the novel. Divakaruni retells Mahabharata from Draupadi's perspective. Those who are interested in Indian epic must read this novel open mindedly to perceive it in a new light. She gives entire panorama of the epic with minute details. Divakaruni's Draupadi is woman of her own. She is smarter one of the two children of king Drupad. This novel proves that Divakaruni is indeed a storyteller par excellence, no matter what her method.

Memory is very crucial in almost all Diasporic writers. Memory involves the written history. It is the written records of one's experience. They always look back. They preserve their past and try to reconnect their land through writing. Writers like Shashi Tharoor, Vikram Seth, Vikram Chandra, and Salman Rushdie rewrite the history in contemporary terms. *The Great Indian Novel* by Shashi Tharoor is intelligible to readers who have understood the ancient Indian epic *Mahabharata*. The use of myths, archetypes in Diasporic writing shows the obsession of writers to their emotional and cultural roots. Manju Jaidka points out the way Diasporic writers narrate the real world and imaginary world in their fiction:

> In the fictional world of diaspora writers we have, thus, Utopias and anti-Utopias, real worlds and the imaginary. The demarcating lines are faint: the different worlds blend and merge so that they are not easily distinguishable, and the perspectives keep shifting. These worlds are a mix of memory and desire-memory of a bygone time and, perhaps, the desire to regain the same. The method of their portrayal varies: it may be realism, naturalism, or magic-realism, each writing style being unique in its own way. Yet, even though these diverse worlds differ with individual writers, certain characteristics remain common in all. (29)

REFERENCES

1. Bhattacharjee Sukalpa, "The Text as Narrative: Reading Ideology", *Ethnic Literatures of America Diaspora and Intercultural Studies* ed. by Somdatta Mandai, Himardri Lahiri, Prestige Books 2005, p. 46.
2. *http://www.pathfindes.com/time/magazine/1997/int/970811/spl.neighbors.html*
3. Kapadia Novy, "Expatriate Experience and Theme of Marriage in *An American Braf*', *The Novels of Bapsi Sidhwa*. ed. R. K. Dhawan and Novy Kapadia, Prestige, 1996.
4. Paranjape R. Makarand, "The Novels of Bapsi Sidhwa", *The Novels of Bapsi Sidhwa* ed. R. K. Dhawan and Novy Kapadia, Prestige, 1996, p. 88
5. Kapadia Novy, "The Parsee Paradox in Bapsi Sidhwa's "The Crow Eaters" *Novels of Bapsi Sidhwa* ed. R. K. Dhawan and Novy Kapadia, Prestige 1996, p. 117
6. Narendrakumar V. L. V. N., "The Twain Shall Meet: Bapsi Sidhwa's Novels", *Parsee Novel*, Prestige 2002, p. 60
7. Kanaganayakam, Chelva, "Interview with Bapsi Sidhwa. *The Toronto South Asian Review*, Vol. II No. 1, summer, 1992, p. 46
8. Hai Ambreen, "Border work, Bourder trouble: Postcolonial Feminism and The Ayah in Bapsi Sidhwa's *Cracking India"*. *Modern Fiction Studies* summer 2000 Vol. 46 pub. John Hopkins University Press, p. 407.
9. *Ibid.*, p. 408.
10. Tripathi Vanashree, "Ambiance of The Backyard And The Dark Corners of History: Bapsi Sidhwa's *Ice-Candy Man" Punjab University Research Bulletin* (arts) Vol XXVI, No 142, April-Oct 1995 ed Moahn maharishi, Punjab University Chandigarh, PP. 116-117.
11. Karafilis Maria, "Crossing the Borders of Genre: Revisions of the Bildungsroman in Sandra Cisneros's The House on Mango Street and Jamaica Kinchid's Annie John", *The Journal of the Midwest Modern Language Association* 1998, p. 65.
12. Paranjape makarand, "The Novels of Bapsy Sidhwa", *The Novels of Bapsi Sidhwa* ed. R. K. Dhawan and Novy Kapadia, Prestige, 1996, p. 81.
13. Sukalpa Bhattcharjee. "The Text as Narrative: Reading Ideology", *Ethinic Literatures of America Diaspora and Intercultural Studies* ed. by Somdatta Mandal, Himardri Lahiri, Prestige Books 2005 p. 47

14. Rushdi, Salman, "*Imaginary Homelands: Essays and Criticism 1981-91*". ed. Salman Rushdie. Granta Books in association with Penguin and Books, India, 1991, p. 15
15. Lowe, Lisa. "Immigrant Acts: on Asian American Cultural Politics" *Durhan NC*: Duke Up 1996, p. 164.
16. Wong, Sau-ling, C, "Middle Class a Global Frame: Refiguring the status of Liberty in Divakaruni and Minatoya" *MELUS*. The Journal of the society for the study of the Multi-Ethnic Literature of the United States. Guest ed. Amritjit and C. Lok Chua, Vol. 29, No. 3 and 4, Fall/winter 2004, p. 205
17. Eswari C. N., "Post-colonialism Chitra Banerjee's *Sister of My Heart*" Contemporary Literary *Criticism: Theory and Practice* Vol. II, ed. NDR Chandra. Author press, 2003, p. 338.
18. Barat Urbashi, "*Sister of My Heart*: Female Bonding in fiction of Chitra Banerjee Divakaruni. *The Diasporic Imagination. Asian American Writer*. Vol. 1-2, Fiction: Novels and Short Stories ed. Somadatta Mandal, Prestige Books. New Delhi 2000, p. 53
19. Johnson Sarah Anne, "Writing Outside the Lines", *The Writer* Boston: March 2004. Vol. 117, p. 3
20. *Ibid.*, p. 2
21. *Ibid.*, p. 4
22. *Ibid.*, p. 5
23. Zaleski Jeff, "*The Vine of Desire*", *Publisher Weekly* New York, Nov. 26, 2001 Vol. 248, p. 38
24. Steinberg, Sybils. *Publisher Weekly*, New York Jan 13, 1997, Vol. 244, p. 51
25. Banerjee Debjani, "Homo and US: Re-defining Identity in the South Asian Diaspora Through the Writings of Chitra Banerjee Divakaruni and Meena Alexander". *The Diasporic Imagination Asian American Writer*. Vol. 2 Fiction: Novels and Short Stories ed. Somadatta Mandal. Prestige Books New Delhi, 2000, p. 28
26. Johnson Sarah Anne, "Writing Outside the Lines", *The Writer Boston*: March 2004. Vol. 117 p. 3
27. Anonymous, *The Conch Bearer*, *Publishers Weekly*, New York: Aug 18, 2003, Vol. 250, p. 80
28. *http://www.chitradivakaruni.com/books/queenofderams*
29. Jaidka Manju, "The writer as Trishanku : Indian Writing in a foreign Space", *The Diasporic Imagination. Asian American Writing*, Vol. 3, ed. Somdatta Mandal, Prestige 2002, pp. 20-22.

Chapter 5

Conclusion

The South Asian American literature is developing as a new field of study. It is considered one of the subdivisions of multicultural literature. Asian American writers have flourished over the years as they express their ethnic identity, the interrelations, intricacies, and contradictions that make up Asian America. Today many are receiving the attention and praise that have been long overdue. The recent explosion of literature from Asian American writers shows that there is an abundance of topics and issues to be covered. There is no single "Asian American Experience", as there exists the political, socioeconomic, and cultural diversity among Asian Americans. Their collective and unique experiences form a mosaic that unites world, instead of dividing it.

The present research work takes note of the South Asian American literature in general and an Indian Immigrant woman's writing in particular. In the contemporary scene of letters, it is an undeniable fact that almost all the major Indian writers in English write from diaspora spaces in the west. The triumphant moment for expatriate Indian writing in English can be dated to 1981 when Rushdie's *Midnight's Children* was published. For the Indian Writing English these two and a half decades have been a defining moment, a triumphal moment, and mainly on account of the achievement of the expatriate Indian Writings.

Literature of diaspora reveals the different patterns of migration. Almost all literary fiction today are cultural fictions which are written from the affective experience of social marginality, from disjunctive, fragmented, displaced agency and from the perspective of the edge. The literature of diaspora is an attempt to produce an act of reinscribing, of revising and hybridizing the settled discursive hierarchies by constructing third space beyond existing political, social and cultural binaries: it is a space of revaluation.

The expatriate Indian writers are not a monolithic category and cannot be viewed as a single homogeneous group. It is essentially a composite cultural context drawing from different nations, cultures and societies. The only single thread running through them is their Indian background. But even the sense of homelessness is not the same thus both memory and homeland acquire multiple meanings in these contexts. Though they share common history, culture and spiritual belief; the responses of individual's writers vary widely. There are some expatriate writers who like V. S. Naipaul insist on an identity that is shaped by exile, loss and the vast betrayals of history. In contrast writers like Bharti Mukherji believes a complete assimilation with the adopted land would be the answer to the discontents of the diaspora. And there are writers such as Salman Rushdie who celebrate the old and the new, India and the diaspora, our myths and our realities. Writers like Jhumpa Lahari, Hari Kunzru, who grew up in foreign land – have announced their desire not to be classified as Indian writers. For Kunzru, India is simply a country where his relatives live and where he occasionally comes for family weddings and holidays. But always at the core of expatriate writing there is a haunting presence of motherland.

There are three generations of Indian women writers who wrote from locations outside their homelands. The first generation of these writers includes writers like Santha Rama Rau, Attia Hossain and Kamala Markandaya, all of who migrated in the Forties. Their work is important in historicizing postcolonial diasporas. The next generations of writers include writers like Bharti Mukherjee, Suniti Namjoshi, Leena Dhingra, Indira Ganesan, Chitra Divakaruni, and Meena Alexander. These writers describe multiple patterns of diasporic movement motivated by different factors: interracial marriage, mobile parents or preference for alternative sexualities. These writers use gender and sexuality as sites of diasporic negotiations in interrogating racist, nationalist and traditional discourses enclosing them.

A close analysis of the texts of Bapsi Sidhwa and Chitra Banerjee brings out the fact that the lives of their protagonists which are in flux are symbolic of Indian subcontinental diaspora. Expatriate women writers from the South Asian Diaspora reconstruct subcontinental history in their writing. Women move from village to town, from one country to another for a variety reasons. Sometimes they join a husband who has gone ahead to look for prospects; sometime they go on their own to earn more; sometime time they are forced to face to move because of war, famine, poverty or political persecution. Their move may be forceful or voluntary, it is not easy one. The situation which they have to face after migration is beyond their control. Today, half of all international migrants are women. The state of the world's population 2006, the annual assessment of population Fund, has focused this time on women and international migration. When women whatever class, are forced by circumstances to migrate, they expose themselves to new forms of violence and exploitation. Though the reality is harsh, protagonist of Divakaruni and Sidhwa fight against all odds and tell their successful stories of assimilation.

Both Chitra Banerjee and Bapsi Sidhwa are good storytellers. They do not disconnect their lives from the historical past like Bharti Mukherjee to become main stream American writers. On the contrary, they believe – it is their tradition, history, memory and ethnicity, which help them to re-root in the foreign land. So like typical migrant novelist, both Sidhwa and Divakaruni bring "modern" worlds and "old" worlds together in their writing. In their fictional world we have, thus different worlds jostling each other, real world and the imaginary. The demarcating lines are faint: the two spheres blend and merge so that they are not easily distinguishable. These worlds are mix of memory and desire – memory of a bygone time and perhaps the desire to regain the same. To understand the complexity of the problem of diaspora they break the realist unities of time and space. Their novels are 'translated' and they show a constant interaction of style, voices, stories, legends and geographies. Lata Rengachari has rightly pointed the alternative narrative these women writers have provided:

> They also practice what Gayatri Spivak calls the 'frontier style' favouring cross-hatched, fragmented, and choric forms. The story telling is self-consciously many voiced, or interrupted and digressive in the manner of the oral tale. This writing combines epistolary address, songs, dramatic interchanges, all techniques that work against the unifying viewpoint more typical of European realism, and the nationalist novels by male writers. (1)

Displacement and migration within the country or outside the country has become the contemporary trend in almost all countries because of the changed global economic, political and cultural scenario. Contemporary homelessness is translated into fiction. Today, an individual owns several homes, which empowers him rather than weaken. Dislocation has provided alternative locations to migrants. The intensity of diasporic experience is changing with time. Divakaruni and Sidhwa have shown through their fiction – the way diasporic experiences are changing. The migrant diaspora in the beginning, experience the pangs of displacement, fragmentation, marginalization, cultural dilemmas and the generational differences. But later on we see changes in them. These migrants live together, as a community in the foreign country. They try to preserve their culture in language, religion, custom or folklore. Avtar Brah describes the status of Diasporas in the dominant culture. She says:

> ....all Diasporas are differentiated, heterogeneous, contested paces, even as they are implicated in the construction of a common 'we' (2)

Thus, it is clear that diaspora discourse has often made assumptions about dislocation and homelessness; these assumptions are reversed by the changing situation of individuals in the multicultural contests. Mongrelization and heterogeneity seem to define the contempororary condition of the succeeding generation of the immigrant parents. The transnational technological networks enabled them set up close linkages with their homeland. This is the age of in-betweeners. In course of time, diaspora individuals from the same country form communities and different diaspora communities make "Composite Communities". Thus transnational communities are formed. According Robin Cohen the distinct diaspora communities are constructed out of "the confluence of narratives of the old country to the new, which create the sense of shared history" (3)

Homi Bhabha's theories figure prominently in the earlier chapters. Bhabha's concept of hybridity is a complex one, applicable not merely to identity, but also to theory and discourse. His theory of cultural hybridity (1994) recognizes all cultural relations as ambivalent, subversive, transgressive and hybrid. To Bhaba, hybridity is not a thing but a process. Hybridity does not comprise of two original moments from which the third emerges but points out to an ambivalent third space of cultural production and reproduction. Hybridity as posited by Bhabha has been helping to understand varied experiences of contemporary diaspora. In *The Location of Culture*, Bhabha observes how 'difference' disturbs hegemonic discourses, which discriminate and exercise their power over the suppressed. But Bhabha also points out that from the point of view of the suppressed cultures, "difference" forces a confrontation, an opposition and brings about a resistance. The protagonists of Bapsi Sidhwa and Chitra Banerjee change during their stay in the new country. They constantly intervene the dominant culture and interrogate their own culture to carve their own route in the new country. Thus, "hybrid identities" are born. These changed identities no doubt lead to further conflicts but it certainly opens new routes and mode of thinking for the individual and group identities of Diasporas and guides them to outgrow the stereotyped experiences of uprootedness, displacement and marginalization. Thus, the margins or 'in-between' space has given a platform to immigrant women to tell their stories. Writers like Sidhwa and Divakaruni feel that they can observe their home country and the adopted country objectively. Their immigrant experience has explored their creativity and made them writer.

Explorations of alternative histories, interrogation of the master code and rewriting of histories have been central concerns of the many expatriate Indian Writers. Typically, the tendency of the expatriate writer is also to project contemporary history through myth, allegories and parody. What is significant about Divakaruni and Sidhwa is they also write about the contemporary history. Divakaruni has written a novel – *Queen of Dreams* on a national tragedy of 9/11 and its repercussion on the existence of Asian Communities, especially in the United States. Sidhwa, being Parsi is the third person observer and the witness of the partition of India and Pakistan. She takes up these issues in almost all her novels.

In her recent interviews Sidhwa openly discussed about the paradoxes of American policies. After 9/11, she urges Muslims not to leave America and show them what the real Islam is. All her novels give the live picture of the migration of the historically diasporic Parsee community and their process of assimilation. The novel *An American Brat* can prove to be a good handbook for the Third World migrants to US. Manek, an uncle of protagonist Feroza has given her all lessons of assimilation. In this novel the Zoroastrian worldview operates explicitly. The heightened consciousness of Feroza is the outcome of expatriation. Her intense search for adequate social space in the New World is typical of an expatriate, since she too faces rejection in the white man's land, though initially.

As this New World alone ensures her satisfaction, happiness coupled with freedom, she decided to settle in America. Thus like Freddie in *The Crow Eaters*, Feroza succeeds in attaining social status and prosperity on the alien land. Through the triumph of Feroza and Freddie, Sidhwa shows-by preserving ethnic identity one can easily settle in the foreign country. Both Freddie and Feroza are typical migrants who practice the values of charity and adaptability. Thus for both, Feroza and Freddie, the chosen land (America and Lahore) provides adequate social place to grow and attain prosperity and success whereas Zoroastrianism continues to provide enough emotional and religious space. In almost all Parsee novels in English, the Zoroastrian worldview thus acts as a driving force and provides an excellent medium for adaptability. Divakaruni has also shown through her characters-the way Indian culture, tradition has helped them to settle in America.

Recently, Sidhwa has published an anthology on Lahore. The title of the book is-*City of Sin and Splendor: Writing on Lahore*. She has published the book-*The Mouse with Seven Tails* for children. In her recent interview with Banibrata Mahanta, Sidhwa talked about her new projects. She has also written novel on Deepa Mehta's film *Water*. Deepa Mehta is thinking of making *The Crow Eaters* into a movie. Like Divakaruni, she is not only a writer but also a social worker. She has her association with the social work organization, *Pratham,* which does a lot of fund raising in America.

Life is full of paradoxes. Sidhwa's writing helps us to accept these paradoxes with humour. Sidhwa is the first Pakistani writer to be published in English. Sidhwa comments:

> Yes and that's not just in Pakistan but in India also. I have written differently. Humor, fun, which no women had done. Even now they don't do it. (4)

By taking the advantage of her hyphenated identity, Sidhwa dares to talk against the interventionist policies of the US administration. She says:

> Well, the United States itself is now very divided. The only think they are united in is the hate against Muslims.

> They have demonized Muslims because America always needs to have somebody to hate. You know, it's the glue that holds the country together. Hate and fear. First it was hate and fear of communism and communists. That's finished. Now they need to hate somebody else, its Islam and Muslim countries. (5)

Today world is becoming increasingly multicultural; Sidhwa is the most hybridized writer. She comments on her multicultural identity:

> I wouldn't put it that way. I am first of all a Parsi, then I am Punjabi, then I am Pakistani and Indian because I have been the citizen of India also Bombay is my home. That's where all the Parsis live. So I define myself as well these. And now I am living in America. For me now, borders have become meaningless. I have lost that sense of patriotism that I once had. I feel patriotism leads to all sorts of divisions between you and me. I'd rather be a citizen of all the countries that I know. I can't say I am a citizen of world because I don't know the world. But I certainly am a citizen of the subcontinent and now of America. I have published a lot in Italy so I have also come to know Italy a bit. (6)

Similarly, Divakaruni shows through her writing that the construction of these new identities is a matter of 'becoming' or negotiation with host society. Divakaruni's fiction deals with the theme of immigrant conflict – acquired values versus adopted ones. It is very difficult to write about two different worlds. Divakaruni, talked about the process of assimilation in an adopted land to Uma Girish. She says:

> It's okay to be an Indian person who loves Indian culture but now I am an American citizen and committed to making life in this country better. We need to remain secure in our own identity but participate fully in the culture, politics and daily life of America. The important part of integration is that you don't give up, you share. For me as a writer a major challenge is to keep my finger on the pulse of both worlds. That means talking to people on

> continents, observing them, learning what is changing with them and remains the same. This also means that I am writing for audiences that are very different. This is difficult, especially as I refuse to explicate culture. (7)

Changes in the world since 1989 have refocused attention on the displaced person, the migrant and the stranger, people dispossessed and separated from their identity and their history. This experience is seen in the context of a new global economy. Today human expectations have changed. International law provides protective cover and the consciousness of human rights has increased all over the world. Though all democratic countries believe in multiculturalism as a value, the power or hegemony remains a constant factor which characterizes the relationship between individuals, peoples or nations. Multiculturalism is an irreversible fact today, although the multiculturalists societies in the US, Canada and Britain have, of late, in the wake of the events of 9/11 and 7/7, begun to seriously question their commitment to pluralism as a way of life. Divakaruni and Sidhwa take note of these issues and their fiction deals with the ever changing lived reality of cultural dynamics in the Diasporic experience in all its specifics. Divakaruni believes that her intercultural writing will promote a dialogue between Indians and non-Indians:

> Intercultural writing is a great thing. It has always been a good thing and will continue to be, no matter if someone decides it's "in" or not. Reading about other cultures, about lives very different from our own, expands us as human beings. I don't simplify from where I come from. I try to lure readers of all backgrounds with the characters and the story. If the writing is good then readers will identify. If one approaches a book with attention, one gets a lot out of it intuitively. I hope my books will promote conversations and discussions between Indians and non-Indians. (8)

Thus the Diasporic writing by Chitra Divakaruni, Bapsi Sidhwa, Farrukh Dhondy and Amitav Ghosh, need not to be defined in the stereotyped categories of loss and anguish, it represents the agony of all marginalized communities from the world. They want to come out of post colonial perspectives to move into a larger, humanistic discourse where cultural values are translated.

As people are crossing borders time to time, their sense of patriotism is also changing and must change. As Sidhwa is citizen of many countries, her patriotism is not confined to one country. Today we see patriotism is giving birth to terrorism. Multiculturalism as a value of democratic country is getting publicity now a days. The margin centre relationship is not stable. In this age of Information technology, it is said that the world is becoming a global village and borders are becoming meaningless. It is also said that we are the citizen of the world. But people are dwindling into symbols. Ironically, in the face of global technology and the impact of satellite communications, ethnicity is becoming last refuge into which great masses all over the world are coming back. Nilufer Bharucha has rightly pointed, "That in a postcolonial, postmodernist, post Marxist world, most human beings ultimately live in tribal mansions."(9) According to Jasbir Jain, "there are two possibilities. One is the dangerous trend towards hardening of attitudes, a withdrawal, hostility- the newfound fundamentalism which lurks behind the new face of modernism. And the other is the possibility of a new humanist discourse emerging out of the new vibrancy of ethnicity."(10)

Sidhwa and Divakaruni try to bring the world together through their writing. Their writing is a new humanist discourse emerging out of the new vibrancy of ethnicity, which is in flux. Both Sidhwa and Divakaruni consider their writing as the spiritual process. Today entire social milieu is changing because of globalization and technology. Migration has become the part of people's life. The literature of Diaspora, which is emerging rapidly, is the need of time as it helps to develop the cross-cultural understanding. Both Bapsi Sidhwa and Chitra Banerjee help to develop the skills of assimilation among the migrants all over the world through their writing.

REFERENCES

1. Rangachari; Latha, "Debating Expatriate Women's writing from the Indian Subcontient" *The Diasporic Imagination. Asian American writing.* Vol. 3. ed. Somdatta Mandal. Prestige, p. 36.
2. Brah Avtar, *Cartographies of Diaspora: Contesting Identities* Routledge, 1997, p. 184.
3. Cohen Robin, *Global Diasporas: An Introduction.* UCI Press, 1997, p. ix.
4. Mahanta Banibrata, "Interview with Bapsi Sidhwa", *The Journal of Indian writing In English,* Vol.34. July 2006 No. 2, p. 52.
5. *Ibid.*, p. 51.
6. *Ibid.*, p. 53
7. Girish Uma, "Straddling Two Cultures". *http://www.calitreview.com/Interview int divakaruni 8002.htm.*
8. *Ibid.*, p. 2.
9. Bharucha Nilufer, "Resisting Colonial and Postcolonial Hegemonies: Bapsi Sidhwa's Ethno-Religious Discourse". *Asian American Writing* Vol. 17. ed. Somanath Mandal, Prestige Books New Delhi 2000, p. 83.
10. Jain Jasbir, "Political Realities and the Colours of Imagination". *Ethnic Literatures of America.* Diaspora and Intercultural studies ed. Somdatta Mandal, Himadri Lahiri. Prestige. 2005, p. 31.

Index

A

A Perfect Life, 94
Abba, 80
Adoption, 95
Affair, 150
Affair, 91
Ahuja, 104
Akbar, 68
Alexander, Meena, 86
Amchur, 105
American Born Confused Desi, 120
American Brat, 143
American campus life, 58
American Jew David Press, 63
Amla, 107
An American Brat, 25, 26, 47
Anglo-Indians, 72
Anju, 118, 160
Aparana, US, 100
Appachana, Anjan, 34
Arranged Marriage (1995), 2
Arranged Marriage, 33, 88
Asafetida, 106
Asha, 69
Ashoka, 68
Asian American Experience, 166

B

Banerjee, Chitra, 132-165
Banyan tree, 6
Bhabha, Homi, 87
Bhartiya Pravasi Divas, 4
Bharucha, 78
Bhutto, 49, 50
Brain Gain, 4
British Raj, 74
Brotherhood conch, 128
Bye-bye Blackbird (1971), 51

C

California, 153
Candy man, 145
Chicago, 93
Chris, 95
Christian, 60
Cinnamon, 107
Clear Light of Day, 41
Clothes, 89
Commonwealth Writers Prize, 2

Composite Communities, 170
Conch Bearer, 125
Consciousness, 16
Cosmopolitanism, 15
Cracking India, 25, 75
Crime, 53
Culture and Imperialism, 13
Cyberspace, 3

D

Daruwalla, Keki N., 79
Democracy, 29
Desai, Anita, 1
Diana, 106
Diasporas, 169
Divakaruni, Chitra Banerjee, 40, 86
Divorce, 62
Doors, 96
Draksha, 106
Drapud, 163
Draupadi, 124
Dutta, 98

E

Émigrés and refugees, 8
Europeans, 72
Exile, 5
Expatriation, 54

F

Faithful Sita, 92
Farukh, 82
Fear, 57
Feroza, 134
Feroza, 49
Flexibility, 144
Foothill College, 33
Foreign citizen, 88
Freddy for short, 68
Freedom, 91
Fun, 172

G

Gandhari, 124
Gandhi, 77
Gatherings of exiles, 8
Gauri, 110
Gayatri Spivak, 10
Geeme a lemonade, 135
Geeta, 105
Ghalib, 145
Girish, Uma, 173
Girls Many Land series, 124
Globalization and technology, 175
Globalization, 18
Good man, 100
Government of Pakistan, 25
Great Men women, 137
Greece and Rome, 99
Griffiths, 51, 79
Gundaas, 49

H

Harry Potter, 125
Hindu(s), 7, 60, 72
Hira Mandi, 72
Hubs of Poverty, 55
Humor, 172

I

Ice-Candy-Man, 19, 146
Imiginary Homelands, 14
Immigrant, 5
Indian Diaspora, 3

Indian National Congress, 74
Indian Nationalist, 77
Indian Prince, 21
Indian writing English, 166
Internet, 103
Introduction, 1-45
Iqbal, 145
Islam, 171

J

Jaidka, Manju, 163
Jasmine, 11
Jasmine, 94
Jo, 134

K

Kalapani, 105
Kris, 95
Kunti, 124
Kusti, 64

L

Language, 169
Lexington Avenue, 59
Literature of Diaspora, 175
Little Women, 18
Lofar, 107
Love and luck, 156
Love of Good Man, 99

M

Magic realism, 157
Mahabharata, 36, 124, 163
Maitri, 34
Manek, 171
Manvi, 37
Marginalization, 147
Markandaya, Kamala, 167
Marlowe, Christopher, 32
Martial law, 50
Marxist world, 175
Meena, 90
Meeting Mrinal, 92, 150
Memory, 47, 163
Midnight Children, 166
Migrants, 169
Mirror of Fire and Dreaming, 127
Mormon territory, 58
Morrison, Toni, 148
Mukherjee, Bharti, 143
Mullahs, 49, 65
Multitude, 88
Muslim villagers, 47
Muslim, 50, 60, 78

N

Naik, M.K., 1
Naipaul, 14
Narayan, R.K., 1
Nation and Narration, 92
Nationalism, transnationalism, liminality, 46-85, 86-131
    diasporic experience in Bapsi Sidhwa, 46-83
Native art, 132-165
Nawabs, 69
New world, 50, 171
Nigger, 33

O

Oppression, 147

P

Pakistan Army in 1971, 33

Pakistan, 18
Palace of Illusion, 124
Pandavas, 4
Pantheon of gods and angels, 8
Parekh, Bhikhu, 6
Parsi ethnicity, 54
Paris/Zoroastrian community, 46
Parsee, 21, 48, 60, 70
Parsee Community in Lahore, 49
Patras Bokhari Award for Literature in Pakistan, 25
Pratham, 172
Privacy, 144
Promised Land, 54

Q

Quasim, 81
Queen of Dreams, 33, 119, 123, 171

R

Rajas, 69
Ramayana, 36
Random House, 1
Recasting women, 83
Religion, 169
Resistance, 147
Roy, Arundhati, 2
Roy, Ashwarya, 109
Rushdie, 14
Rushdie, Salman, 2

S

Sachidanand, K., 7
Secularism, 62
Selfess Kunti, 92
Sen, Amartya, 10
Sen, Nabaneeta Dev, 37
Seth, Vikram, 1
Shadowland, 127
Shakespeare, 40
Sidhwa, Bapsi, 17, 27, 46, 132-165, 170, 171
Sikh, 60
Silver Pavements and Golden Roofs, 93
Singh, Gurubhat, 14
Sister of My Heart, 36, 110
Skahi, 37
Smith, Anthony, 7
Sour Sweet, 51
Space of revaluation, 167
Spiritual belief, 167
Srimad Valimik Ramayana, 125
Statue of Liberty, 55, 95
Such a Long Journey, 2
Sudha, 153
Sudra, 64
Sumita, 90
Sympathetic, 137

T

Terrorist, 121
The Bride here, 23
The Bride, 80, 146
The Chai House, 120, 121
The Conch Bearer, 161
The Crow Eaters, 19, 71, 172
The God of Small Things, 2, 31
The Golden Gate, 2
The Great Indian Novel, 163
The Interpreter of Maladies, 2
The Lives of Strangers, 99
The Location of Culture, 10, 90, 128, 170

The Mistress of Spices, 32, 38, 101, 104, 108, 109, 156

The Pakistani Bride, 23, 48, 134

The Queens of Swords, 150

The Ramayana, 7

The Reasons for Nasturiums, 33

The Shock of Arrival, 93

The Unknown Errors of our Lives, 98, 100

The Vine of Desire, 33, 114, 116, 117, 152

The Woman Warrior, 40

Third World, 157, 171

Tilo, 102

Train to Pakistan, 75

Trishanku, 7

Twin Falls, 58

U

United States, 48, 171

University of Denver, 58

USA, 2

V

Vine of Desire, 31

Voltaire Candide, 24

W

Water, 172

Woolf, Virginia, 114, 158

World-wide welcome, 95

Wright State University in Ohio, 32

Y

YMCA, 56

Z

Zarathushtra, 71

Zareen, 64

Zoroastrian, 19, 21, 70

Zoroastrianism, 145

Zoroastrians, 171

Zurvan mythic face, 61